MUSINGS ON HUMAN METAMORPHOSES

TIMOTHY LEARY

RONIN PUBLISHING
BERKELEY, CA

Musings on Human Metamorphoses
ISBN: 1-57951-058-2
Copyright © 1988 by Timothy Leary
Copyright © 2003 by Futique Trust

Published by
RONIN Publishing, Inc.
PO Box 22900
Oakland, CA 94609
www.roninpub.com

Credits:

Editor:	**Beverly A. Potter** www.docpotter.com
Copy Editor:	**Amy Demmon**
Cover Painting:	**David Cabot** CabotArt@cs.com
Cover Design:	**Brian Groppe** bagroppe@bellsouth.net
Fonts - cover:	Stardust by T-26
	Hoeffler by Hoeffler
	Roughwork by Scriptorium
	Giza by Agfa
Fonts - text:	Gouty Old Style by URW
	Hot Coffee by Fonthead Design
	Jolly Jack by Fonthead Design
	Keener by Fonthead Design www.fonthead.com
	Turkey Sandwich by John Martz jmartz@sentex.net

Distributed to the trade by **Publishers Group West**
Printed in the United States of America by **Arvato**
Library of Congress Card Number: 2002096223
Printing Number 1

Note: Material in the book was excerpted from
Changing My Mind Among Others (1988) by Timothy Leary.

TABLE OF CONTENTS

FOREWORD

BY PAUL DAVIDS

TWO GREAT PHILOSOPHIC QUESTIONS have challenged all human beings since the invention of rational thought: Where do we come from? Where are we going? In *Musings on Human Metamorphoses*, Timothy Leary weighs in on both of these philosophic challenges with the same one-word answer to each—*Space*.

It was a symbolic act, when Timothy Leary decided that seven grams of his ashes would be blasted into space in a capsule that included some of the ashes of *Star Trek* creator Gene Roddenberry. From space we came, to space we shall return. Timothy pointed the way to our collective destiny and future. He made his actions function as a demonstration of his theories, ideas and beliefs. This, he believed, was a requirement of his profession—*Philosopher*.

In the book you are about to read, Timothy Leary focuses his mind microscope on some of

TIMOTHY POINTED THE WAY TO OUR COLLECTIVE DESTINY AND FUTURE.

the many theories of our existence, from earth-bound evolution to the God hypothesis, from Buddhist nihilism to Marxist atheism. In his unique style he turns to two concepts he believes can reveal the secrets of life and the great cosmic mysteries: higher intelligence and panspermia.

HIGHER INTELLIGENCE

FOR TIMOTHY LEARY, "higher intelligence" means that somewhere out in the recesses of space and within the molecular structure of all that exists, an intelligence is manifest that far surpasses the powers of our meager human brain. He does not call this intelligence "God" in any conventional sense. It could be an ALF—that is, an Alien Life Form, "something" from somewhere "out there." Or higher intelligence could be pervasive throughout space, an intelligent force that manifests in electric discharges and primal forces of nature including light itself.

For Timothy Leary, DNA is the ultimate birthplace and sanctuary of all life, and he gives no ground to those who assume that DNA must have originated on Earth. From the DNA "seed" comes

DNA IS THE ULTIMATE BIRTH-PLACE AND SANCTUARY OF ALL LIFE.

the essence and all future metamorphosis of life. DNA takes whatever forms are possible on whatever worlds it encounters. In an atmosphere of air like the one we are familiar with here on Earth, DNA will enable emerging creatures to evolve lungs. Under oceans, DNA will enable gills to evolve. Who knows what it will evolve—or once did evolve—on Mars or Venus or out in the star system of the Pleaides?

PANSPERMIA

"PANSPERMIA" IS THE SECOND ESSENTIAL CONCEPT explored in this book. Panspermia is the idea that DNA—or the biological molecules that are its precursors—floats throughout the void of space, in asteroids and ice crystals, in space dust and comets. Whatever atmosphere DNA penetrates, whether in our own solar system or in the star system of Alpha Centauri—or even in other galaxies—DNA will weave a tapestry of biological forms that can survive the natural forces of whatever world it comes upon by "chance." That's when "local" evolution begins.

Contained within DNA, Timothy Leary argues, is the blueprint of a Higher Intelligence that not only inwardly directs the course of adaptation to environments of all kinds, but also predetermines the future of living organisms. That future is this: life shall evolve to higher and higher states of intellect, and it shall seek its future free of the constraints of planetary

DNA CONTAINS THE BLUEPRINT OF HIGHER CONSCIOUSNESS.

existence, building artificial worlds—spaceships or space colonies—that travel throughout the void of space itself.

From space we came, to space we shall return. It is our destiny, written in our DNA as our ultimate potential, from a forgotten time long before we evolved from sea creatures and crawled upon the land.

As you will discover in reading this book, the idea that older life forms exist elsewhere in the universe made sense to Timothy Leary. He was far less willing to commit to the notion that these life forms are visiting Earth now in physical form and have been interacting directly with humanity throughout its history.

When I interviewed Timothy for the feature film documentary I directed, and which I produced with Todd Easton Mills, *Timothy Leary's Dead*, I queried him about "alien abduction." With a characteristic twinkle in his eye, he resisted the notion that biological alien "bodies" are being packaged in space-ships by cultures on other star systems and visiting Earth for the purpose of "molesting little old ladies in Iowa," as he put it. When I suggested that aliens might be here for the purpose of experimenting with and manipulating DNA of humans, animals and plants, he allowed for that possibility. But all in all, he was rather a skeptic when it came to the concept that extraterrestrial UFOs may actually "be here now."

COULD UFOS BE HERE NOW?

MY SIGHTING

MY OWN SERIOUS INTEREST in extraterrestrial forms of higher intelligence began in 1987, after a daylight sighting of a flying saucer, that I witnessed at close range from my home with my two children. It became the subject of an article in *International UFO Reporter* and numerous lectures at UFO conferences. Six years after that sighting, my emerging interest in UFOs and ETs had propelled me to executive produce a film for Showtime entitled *Roswell*, starring Martin Sheen, Kyle MacLachlan and Dwight Yoakam. Not to be confused with the TV series of the same title that followed years later, the Showtime film *Roswell* earnestly dramatized the testimony of a group of military men who insisted that an extraterrestrial spaceship crashed near Roswell, New Mexico, in 1947, and that the government has concealed the facts, the evidence, the debris—and the bodies.

Lt. Col. Philip Corso later co-authored a book, *The Day After Roswell*, claiming that many of the technological breakthroughs of our modern world resulted from back-engineering the advanced alien technology from the Roswell craft. The skeptics pounced all over him.

Timothy seemed sufficiently interested in the film *Roswell*—and a series of *Star Wars* books my wife and I wrote for Lucasfilm and Bantam Books—to trust me to become the director of another film that was very personal to him: his life story. We referred to it as "The Life and Times of Timothy Leary" while we were in production, and posthumously it became *Timothy Leary's Dead*, in homage to the lyrics of Ray Thomas' classic song about Leary called, "Legend of a Mind."

A TREASURE

IN WORKING WITH TIMOTHY ON THE FILM, which covered all of his favorite topics, from psychedelics to cryonics, I became determined to do my own part to see that the legend of this particular mind would survive him. Timothy Leary's many books and papers encompass contemporary civilization—its shining moments and dismal failings, modern science, the human brain and futurism. I considered these extensive musings to be a vastly under-appreciated national treasure.

In his book, *Bibliography of the Writings of Timothy Leary*, author Michael Horowitz—father of actress Winona Ryder, who is Timothy Leary's god-daughter—uses three hundred pages merely to list all of Leary's books and papers, giving a page or paragraph to each work. That's a body of writing that approaches the length and scope of the writings of Dr. Sigmund Freud.

Anyone who studies the history of Leary's writings, many of which were accomplished while he was in prison, knows that they have long been suppressed. They have been dismissed and hounded into "out-of-print" status by liberals and conservatives alike, since both sides of the U.S. political spectrum seem to harbor equal disdain for Timothy Leary's brand of original thoughts. His thoughts, to use two clichés, "push the envelope" and are "outside the box." The Establishment likes everything *inside* envelopes and *packaged* in boxes. Thus, Ronin Publishing has begun to do us all the kind service of putting thousands of "Leary-isms" into envelopes and boxes and shipping them to bookstores and homes throughout the world. What a turn-on!

QUESTION AUTHORITY

TIMOTHY LEARY QUESTIONED AUTHORITY—in fact, he questioned *everything*—qualifying him as a major troublemaker. During the era of political paranoia and heightened militarism of the Vietnam War, his clarion call to "Turn On, Tune In and Drop Out" wasn't the message that those in power wanted to promote. Quite the opposite. Thus, forces were set in motion to "get Timothy Leary"—to arrest him for whatever reason at whatever cost, put him in solitary confinement, and take his typewriter away from him. Without a typewriter, he used a pencil. He refused to complain. "Before Guttenberg invented moveable type, we all used pencils—or quill pens," he said.

TIM QUESTIONED EVERYTHING.

The story of how he was sentenced to decades in prison for possession of two joints of marijuana—and for escape from a low security men's penal colony in California—is well known. The judge who finally "put him away" declared in open court that bail was inappropriate because Leary's ideas and writings were "dangerous." This was justice in the "Land of the Free" in the late 1960s, in the nation busy sacrificing 50,000 of its young men in uniform so that the South Vietnamese could live in freedom from Communism.

Ronin Publishing is committed to the principle that Leary's "dangerous" ideas should live on, without suppression. In creating the Leary Library, Ronin has declared war on the politicians who persecuted Leary and locked him up—a war that is easier to win now that most of those men are mercifully dead, not unlike the current status of Timothy Leary himself. However, thanks to the efforts of Ronin, Timothy Leary will live on in a way that his suppressors will not.

THE MIND YOU EXPAND MAY BE YOUR OWN.

Another philosopher once said that there is nothing so hard to kill as an idea whose time has come. In this book and the others of the Leary Library, you will find quite a few ideas that have been very hard for the Establishment to kill.

I, for one, think that their time has come. Proceed at your own risk—the mind you expand may be your own.

—Paul Davids

CHAPTER 1
COSMIC
gARDENERS

THE THEORIES PRESENTED HERE are science fiction: Scientific in that they are based on empirical findings, fictional in the Wittgensteinian sense that all theories and the speculations beyond the propositions of natural science are subjective.

Christian theologians, statistical materialists, and Marxist dialecticians make different interpretations of the same corpus of scientific fact. Such theories, however popular, are not necessarily any less fictional than those which are persecuted and censored. Indeed, science fictions are forcibly suppressed only when likely to contribute more knowledge and freedom than the defensive orthodoxies they challenge. Think of Socrates, Darwin, Copernicus, Galileo, Pasteur, and the Jehovah's Witnesses in Spain.

Sir Francis Crick, the Nobel laureate who deciphered the DNA code, and his colleague Orgel triggered off a wonderful, life-changing insight. Crick and

EXTRATERRESTRIAL INTELLIGENCE COULD HAVE SENT DNA-SEED PACKETS OUT THROUGH SPACE TO PLANT LIFE ON HOSPITABLE PLANETS, SUCH AS EARTH.

Orgel provided evidence, and much convincing speculation, to support the notion of "directed panspermia." It is possible and feasible, they suggested, that extraterrestrial intelligence at a level of scientific sophistication about equal to our own, could have sent DNA-seed packets out through space to plant life on hospitable planets, such as our Earth.

This was the first intelligent human-level scientific life-origin explanation I ran across, and it clicked. If we domesticated primates could figure out how to seed plants, then intelligent life in other solar systems could have used this obvious gardening technique to perpetuate itself across the galaxy.

DNA SEEDS

ACCORDING TO NEUROLOGIC COSMOLOGY, the planet has already been "invaded" by a superior intelligence to be found in the nervous system and the genetic code. The DNA molecule might be considered a miniaturized, bio-computerized, organic robot, preprogrammed to evolve in optimal reaction to local planetary characteristics.

Life on this planet can be seen as an intelligent information-transmitting process, in which more complex bodies evolve to house more sophisticated nervous systems, until it produces a nervous system capable of using itself as instrument. The general direction of evolution is to produce a serially imprinting, multibrained creature able to decipher its own program, create the technology to leave the planet and live in post-terrestrial mini-worlds, decode the aging sectors of the DNA code—thus assuring immortality, and act in harmony with stages of evolution to come.

THE MISSION IS THE MESSAGE.

From the standpoint of DNA, life is an unbroken chain of simultaneity. Each individual body housing the DNA nucleus is a particle in the wave-rhythm of passage.

GET SMARTER!

Before arrival on this planet, the evolutionary material was already preplanned to evolve serially—imprinting nervous systems that could master planetary survival and explore the message coded within the nervous system and neuron-nucleus.

The mission of DNA is to evolve nervous systems able to escape from the doomed planet and contact manifestations of the same amino-acid seeding that have evolved in other solar systems. The mission is the message—to escape and come home.

DNA IS LIVING INTELLIGENCE

NEUROLOGISTS ASSUME, with primitive insouciance, that studying nerve tissue is no different from the study of the digestive system. Geneticists make the chauvinistic mistake of assuming that DNA is a process, rather than a living intelligence as old as life itself that can teach us the meaning of existence. DNA designs and constructs the nervous system. The mammalian ego, the primate mind, the personality are temporary fragments of the postplanetary nervous system. Neurogeneticists believe

WE ARE THEM.

that the DNA code can communicate revelation and instruction. Our task is to learn how to use the nervous system to receive and modulate DNA's instructions.

Based on all relevant facts from astronomy, genetics, and gerontology the message of DNA is simple: Get Smarter! Increase velocity and altitude! The genetic entity wants off the planet!

UNIVERSE GARDNERS

DISCOVERY OF OVER 30 PRE-BIOTIC ORGANIC MOLECULES floating around in space added support for the theory of panspermia. The work of Sagan, Crick, and the Russian SETI (Search for Extra-Terrestrial Intelligence) experts opened up an exciting chapter in human evolution. Once the concept of extraterrestrial intelligence existed, it was obvious that it will happen. Science tends to find what it starts to look for, so it seemed inevitable that higher intelligence will be found. Either we will contact "them" because we were smart enough to look for "them," or, more likely, we will discover that we are "them" and our species will quickly learn how to seed other planets.

MASTER PLAN

WHAT IS THE MASTER PLAN—AS YOU SEE IT? Your answer determines your life's conduct and meaning. Don't get alarmed, your answer isn't final—you can change it. Perhaps personal evolution recapitulates the history of human philosophy. "Evolve or die" may be true of the individual as well as the species. In asking many people this question, I've discovered that there are four general Master Plan answers.

TRUE BELIEVERS

TRUE BELIEVERS ACCEPT THAT THERE IS A MASTER PLAN and it's all laid down in the Bible, or the Koran, or the book of Mormon, or the Vedas. The Believer's kick is robot obedience, authoritarian certainty. Perform as the rules indicate, and you'll get to heaven. During the Middle Ages, the City of God was the trip. Science, art, human affairs, politics, economics, even survival were irrelevant. A believing culture runs off fear and cannot tolerate questioning, dissent, change.

DARWINIAN HUMANISTS

DARWINIAN HUMANISTS BELIEVE that there is no superhuman intelligence. Evolution is an accidental chance process. Man's mind can progress according to the scientific method of Karl Marx—or Sigmund Freud. The Humanist's kick is success, progress, expansion, competition. Perform as the rules indicate, and you'll win the game. Every day you can improve. Since the Renaissance, humanism has encouraged the middle-classification of science and socialism. Darwin is survival of the fittest. Marx glorifies production.

HINDU HEDONISTS

IN THE HINDU HEDONIST'S VIEW, there is no plan, no progress. Chill out, enjoy yourself. Find the beauty, take care of yourself. The Hedonist's key to life is avoiding tension, conflict, pain, risk. This approach emerges historically when the humanist empire starts to crumble from its own successes and an affluent leisure class begins to look for more than progress. Stoics and Epicureans were most numerous during the latter days of the Roman experiment. For most people, the most intense pleasure is sexual. Sexual liberation occurs when women, freed from economic and social pressures, begin to expect hedonic reward from men, rather than protection.

TO THE ELITIST HEDONIST LIFE IS THE AVOIDANCE OF BOREDOM AND ROUTINE.

The neurological revolution of the 1960s produced Oriental religious movements that preach inner peace, moderation, renunciation of material values, and a self-oriented emphasis on yoga and health regimes. Both *Playboy* and the **LEGALIZE** swami discourage active search for a **FUN!** Master Plan. The elitist, advanced hedonist defines life as the avoidance of boredom and routine. The quest for novelty often leads thoughtful hedonists to search for revelation. *Penthouse*, magazine of the ultra-erotic, sponsors *Omni*, magazine of the slick future.

SCIENTIFIC SEARCHERS

IT IS MOST AMUSING AND LEAST BORING to believe in a Higher Intelligence and a Master Plan. Life is a scientific mystery story, a galactic Whodunit, a Sci-Fi thriller. The Scientific Searcher believes it is possible to decipher the Master Plan for the unfolding of life on this planet. This belief has been nourished for millennia, but persecution has always forced such teachings underground, since the Searcher believes that the better realities are yet to come. This intolerable ultra-evolutionary view implies that "now" is a preparatory phase.

"Atlantis-type" Searchers believe a study of archaeological remnants can reveal lost wisdom. "Extraplanetary" Searchers expect that spaceships will disembark humanoids of higher intelligence, or that a systematic radio-telescope survey of neighboring stars may pick up radio waves.

DECONDITIONING MANTRA

IN THE FIRST DECADE OF THE 20TH CENTURY, occultist Aleister Crowley documented in *The Equinox* his psychological investigations of hashish, concluding that the drug possessed tremendous deconditioning potential. Crowley's "Do what thou wilt shall be the whole of the law" can be a very effective deconditioning mantra for those trapped in certain programmed levels.

REWARD-PAIN CONDITIONING

ACADEMIC PSYCHOLOGY IS CONCERNED with conditioning humans to accept what Freud called the "reality principle," implying that only the artificial, conditioned games of the prevailing social order are real and that natural pleasure is somehow a hallucination—even a psychotic outburst.

Freud's reality principle would be more correctly designated as reward-pain conditioning. You are rewarded for conforming socially and painfully punished if you do not. Reward-pain is real only within the narrow limits of the parochial social order—the hive. Pleasure based on sensory, somatic, cellular, and bioelectrical processes is a reality of another order.

The entire range of pleasurable experiences has gone unstudied, unlabeled, and undefined. You will not find the word "fun" in the index of many psychology texts. Indeed, until the psychedelic movement of the latter 20th Century, unconditioned behavior and unconditioned experience were considered ipso facto schizophrenic. As our society begins to tolerate differing hedonic lifestyles, we can expect an efflorescence of personality systems and psychological models to classify the many varieties of unconditioned, undomesticated hedonic responses.

CROWLEY'S "DO WHAT THOU WILT SHALL BE
THE WHOLE OF THE LAW" CAN BE
A DECONDITIONING MANTRA.

CHAPTER 2
CiRCUiTS oF
MeTAMoRPHoSeS

HOMO SAPIENS EVOLVE THROUGH AN EIGHT-STAGE life cycle or circuits. Each circuit of human metamorphosis produces a life-form visibly different from the preceding and succeeding ones. Each cycle involves dramatic alterations in morphology, behavior, physiology, and—most important—in neurological function.

The nervous system evolves sequentially through eight maturational stages. At each stage, a new circuit emerges. At each chronological stage, a new imprint is taken, determining positive and negative foci for subsequent conditioning of this newly activated circuit.

Though obvious even to the untutored observer, these eight cycles have not been understood by scientists and philosophers. Possibly the human species is itself evolving through the same eight stages, and until recently, has been preoccupied with basic survival processes. By analogy, a caterpillar society would be neurologically inhibited—phylogenetically and individually—from recognizing the butterfly as a later version of itself.

THE FIRST CIRCUIT
BIO-SURVIVAL

THE THEME OF BIO-SURIVIVAL IS "I am safe" and is concerned with safety in a marine environment. The first neural circuit recapitulates the rudimentary nervous system of marine organisms. In the days after birth, the bio-survival imprint fixates basic "approach-avoidance" dimensions of external consciousness, based on dorsal-ventral (front-back) asymmetry. The basic orientation is: Face the positive, avoid the noxious. What is in front is "safe," what is behind is "dangerous."

The first imprint orients one to the mothering person and determines value orientation. If the environment provides food, warmth, quiet, and protection, then a basis is laid for subsequent trustful commerce with the external world. If the human environment of early infancy is unrewarding, cold, painful, and jarring, then the neonate turns its back and does not imprint human beings as the source of safety.

FIRST-CIRCUIT FIXATION

A NEGATIVE FIXATION OF THIS SORT leaves the first neural circuit without a consistent external focus. Result: A persistent inability to relate to the external world. According to this theory, the autistic schizophrenic person can be more usefully diagnosed and treated as first-circuit schizoid, or bio-vegetative schizoid.

According to this theory, the autistic child has imprinted human beings as negative-dangerous, thus preventing learning of human ways. The solution is simple: Suspend the imprint by undoing the biochemical synaptic patterns that define neural circuit programming and make a new imprint involving positive orientation toward the mother.

According to this theory of personality, imprints and conditioned networks can be suspended by the ingestion of LSD, and the person is assured, or assures hirself, in every relevant, truthful way that there is nothing to fear. A calm, serene, courage-inducing environment during reimprinting is the direct "cure."

When used therapeutically, LSD is administered to the autistic child, then the mother or parental person spends eight hours providing the child with warmth, nurturance, tender, soft, and serene stimuli. The new imprinting message is, "We are safe." Three or four such reimprinting experiences combined with consistent post-LSD "safety" stimuli should insure a positive first-circuit conditioning system.

THE SECOND CIRCUIT EMOTION-LOCOMOTION

THE SECOND NEURAL CIRCUIT EVOLVED about 500 million years ago when early Paleozoic vertebrates began to rise up against the pull of gravity. The ability to locomote rapidly and exert superior force became a survival asset, a step towards higher intelligence.

The theme of emotion-locomotion is "I am mobile" and is concerned with territorial security. This midbrain plexus mediates muscular power and gravity mastery. The second circuit imprint occurs when muscular development allows the child to push up and crawl, thus fixating the "above and below" dimensions necessary to deal with the body's vertical head-foot asymmetry. The second imprint combined with the first approach-avoid imprint defines the two-dimensional grid on which all subsequent emotional conditioning is based.

The sympathetic nervous system is triggered by aggression or fear. The young mammal fixates the emotional second-circuit imprint the first time a terror-producing threatening movement occurs and when a smaller, weaker stimulus provokes the predation reflex.

Terror or predation in the mothering person communicates to the child. Subsequently the approach of a snake, a larger animal, a sudden touch arouses the reaction of withdrawal, flight, or anxiety. Similarly, the sight of a small creature running away triggers the preying reflex. Tough or weak behavior attracts adrenaline attention and excites mammalian action.

When faulty imprint or conditioning connects fear and rage with inappropriate situations, a second-circuit schizoid state exists. Selective control of mammalian emotion is the survivally intelligent characteristic. Just as our bio-survival unicellular intelligence is operating quietly at every moment, so does our emotion-locomotion animal nature remain wired for use.

The scary fact is that an overwhelming majority of males alive today would cheerfully rape, loot, and bully any weaker person if the social restraints were temporarily lifted. The emotional circuit is an emergency device. When the human being acts in an emotional way, s/he reverts to a primitive phase of brute power-terror. The basic mammalian "escape them or grab them" reflex still operates today in most of the dictator-run countries of the world.

A MAJORITY OF MALES WOULD CHEERFULLY RAPE, LOOT, AND BULLY ANY WEAKER PERSON IF SOCIAL RESTRAINTS WERE LIFTED.

THE THIRD CIRCUIT
MENTAL-MANIPULATIVE

THE THIRD CIRCUIT IMPRINTS WHEN THE CHILD LEARNS to speak and manifest precise unilateral movements. The theme of the mental-manipulative circuit is "I am right" and is concerned with dexterity, language, and the manufacture of artifacts. It mediates fine, precise muscular activities, especially speech. Dexterity facilitates manipulative grasping (open-close). Thinking is subvocal talking, silent speech.

The emergence of a left cerebral cortex with unilateral dominance has been dated to around two million B.C. when humankind began using stone and bone tools—the beginning of symbolic or substitutive activity.

At the time children begin to speak, they model themselves after adults and peer figures. If the environment is dangerous, restricting, and the parent rejecting, then the child will develop a distrustful, rejecting repetitious mind—perfectly adaptable in a peasant society. By the time the child is five years old, its style of dexterity has been fixed. Later educational exposure, no matter how stimulating, makes little change in the "mind."

THE FOURTH CIRCUIT
SEXUAL-SOCIAL

THE THEME OF THE SEXUAL-SOCIAL CIRCUIT is "I am good" and is concerned with domestication, parenthood, and child-rearing social roles. It mediates activities involved in courtship, strutting, display, mating, copulation, orgasm, as well as family responsibility, social role, and hive membership.

Circuit four activation is marked by dramatic changes in body structure. The fourth-circuit imprint occurs at pubescence, when behavior, thinking, and emotion are dominated by orgasm drive. Other sex-linked factors serve for post-pregnancy protection of mother and young.

The fourth-circuit imprint, combined with the first three, defines the adult or "larval" personality. After impregnation, the fourth-circuit imprint binds the **MOST HUMANS REMAIN AT THE FOURTH LEVEL - DOMESTICATION - THEIR ENTIRE ADULT LIVES.** body to activities connected with the nesting responsibility and nurturance necessary for child survival. Most humans remain at the fourth level of neuro-evolution, i.e., domestication, until menopause leads to the stasis of senility.

EXTERNAL MASTERY

THE FIRST FOUR NEURAL CIRCUITS AND IMPRINTS are totally concerned with preparing the individual to deal with the spatially polarized outside world. The function of the emerging nervous system is to focus, narrow down and choose from an infinity of possibilities—those avenues, spatial tactics, asymmetrical strategies, and **WE PAY A HEAVY PRICE FOR TURF AND SECURITY.** sequences that insure survival. The infant is prepared to imprint any language, master any manipulative intricacy, play any sex role. Without these built-in responses the human infant could not survive.

CHAPTER 3

THE FOUR

FUTIQUE CIRCUITS

THE FIRST FOUR IMPRINTS ARE CONCERNED with mastery of terrestrial turf and insectoid security. For the security of these imprinted realities, however, the human pays a heavy price. Survival and growth in this narrow place means focusing awareness on a trivial fragment of potential experience.

The four post-survival imprints and conditioned networks involve the fabrication of post-terrestrial realities. When the conditioned external survival circuits transcend into the futique circuits, consciousness, which is no longer hooked to the outside, is free to experience the unconditioned pathways of the brain.

Post-planetary time consciousness does not use polarities of terrestrial consciousness. In the Neurological Age of Information, there is no right or wrong; no up or down, no stronger or weaker. There is simply energy in various intensities, durations, qualities, and patterns—signals to be received, changed, selected, filed, retrieved, and harmonized.

DNA MONITORS WHAT HAPPENS TO IT.

The goal of terrestrial consciousness is to survive briefly on a limited planet. The goals of post-planetary consciousness are to evolve and expand in time. Where the four planetary imprints follow laws of Newtonian space physics, the four post-planetary imprints follow laws of Einsteinian time physics.

THE GOAL OF TERRESTRIAL CONSCIOUSNESS IS TO SURVIVE BRIEFLY ON A LIMITED PLANET.

THE FIFTH CIRCUIT
NEURO-SOMATIC RAPTURE

THE THEME OF NEURO-SOMATIC RAPTURE is "I am beautiful" and mediates body-time experience-sensory and somatic, registered by the external sense organs—optical, aural, tactual, taste, smell, temperature, pressure, pain, balance, kinesthetic—and signals from the internal somatic system—breathing, circulation, sex, ingestion, digestion, elimination. Until now, sense organs have served to provide cues for adult, hive-conditioned systems: "Red is for stop; green for go."

THE GOALS OF POST-PLANETARY CONSCIOUSNESS ARE TO EVOLVE AND EXPAND IN TIME.

The rapture imprint occurs the first time direct esthetic impact is received, and "red" and "green" are seen as pulsating light energy. The eye does not "see things," rather it registers direct sensation uninterrupted by mental-manipulative third-circuit thinking. Intensity of sensation is dramatically increased, duration seems longer. Conditioned cues from adult circuits are not wiped out, but harmonized—often humor-ously—with the direct sensations. Consider the modes of meta-rational, polymorphous-erotic perception attained by Fechnerian introspectionists, Zen masters, artists, and entheogen adepts, for example.

PARADOX

IT IS AT THE FIFTH CIRCUIT THAT WE FACE the paradox and terror of time-consciousness. Activating the "silent hemisphere" creates a Hedonic Boom that momentarily shatters all previously imprinted and learned values. Consciousness seems to invade all. The forbidden first-circuit screams, "Danger! Red alert!" The emotion-locomotion second-circuit shouts, "Watch out! You're helpless!" The mental-manipulation third-circuit warns, "Beware! You're in error!" The sexual-social fourth-circuit whispers, "Irresponsible! Violation of sex role!"

THERE IS NO RIGHT OR WRONG, NO UP OR DOWN, NO STRONGER OR WEAKER.

The instinctive terrors mastered by skydivers and circus performers are nothing compared to the momentary panic of a nervous system transcending its four lifelong, life-preserving circuits. We can understand the condemnations of taboo, alienation, stupor, madness, and diabolic possession—as well as the sense of splendid certainty, rebirth, and philosophic exultation accompanying new cortical discoveries made by the courageous, emotionally stable, intellectually prepared, and sexually secure. Discovering the body as instrument of freedom and pleasure is like finding out that a car can be used for pleasure driving. Auto-mobile! Joy-riding the body becomes a hedonic art.

RAPTURE PRONE

EACH SURVIVAL IMPRINT ADDICTS THE NERVOUS SYSTEM to certain external stimuli registered as, or associated with, "positives." Similar addiction occurs in the rapture circuit, where certain organs become "rapture prone," and certain esthetically pleasing sounds, odors, tastes, touches, and somatic reactions become associated with hedonic reward. Rapture can become a satin trap, as the history of decadent leisure classes testifies. Decadence is repetitious indulgence, whereas true self-indulgence is intelligent, flexible, and evolving. Our terrestrial civilizations are overpopulating the globe with insectoid social structures. Exactly at this point, a new generation asks the transcortical questions, "Why? What next?"

DISCOVERING THE BODY AS INSTRU-MENT OF FREEDOM AND PLEASURE IS LIKE FINDING OUT THAT A CAR CAN BE USED FOR PLEASURE DRIVING.

The hedonistic fifth circuit neuro-somatic rapture answer is to "feel good." But the hippie philosophy, however appealing, soon became anti-evolutionary and regressive. The dropout philosophy produced an entire generation of barefoot philosophers, discovering the joyous, infantile delights of direct sensuality. History teaches us that the worship of play and display, eros and beauty is a vulnerable phase, essentially incapable of protecting itself. Woodstock and the French Revolution both teach the lesson: Evolve or perish.

THE SIXTH CIRCUIT

NEURO-ELECTRIC ECSTASY

THE THEME OF NEURO-ELECTRIC ECSTASY is "I create my reality" and mediates neurological time—free of the body and of adult imprints, conscious only of its own functioning. The nervous system literally imprints itself; consciousness is totally composed of neurological signals.

The neuron, the nervous system's anatomical and physiological unit, receives signals via receptor fibers—dendritic fingers—that transmit to the cell body, within which messages are interpreted and stored. The neuron transmits messages to other neurons by squeezing off a chemical secretion that produces a chemical change in the synapse. Basically, the mode of transferring messages across the intercellular gap is a "drug."

Headquarters of the nervous system is, of course, the brain—1,400 grams of nerve tissue floating in a spinal-fluid cushion. Nerve cells do not regenerate. Before birth, the human being possesses 20 billion neurons. That is it. Each day of life, from ten thousand to a hundred thousand cells die—sands of consciousness draining away.

YOU ARE YOUR NERVOUS SYSTEM

HUMAN LIFE IS NOT MEASURED BY THE LIFE SPAN of body cells, which die and regenerate, but by the duration of the nervous system. We are our nervous systems. The body is the car; the nervous system is the driver—an alien, superior **EVOLVE** intelligence residing in the body, which **OR DIE.** it ruthlessly exploits as a means of transportation and supply. Fifty percent of oxygen goes first to the brain. Every neuron is surrounded by glial cells that "taste" and digest all incoming supplies to the regal neuron, like a sultan lying in a warm bath, dealing drugs back and forth.

The nervous system sees no color, feels no pain. Messages from the body are experienced as impulse, buzz, and flash. An experience-addict, the nervous system seeks intensity, novelty, and linkage at high fidelity. Continued change is the diet, high-intensity communication of the longing desire. The person who has emerged into neurological consciousness is capable of simultaneous registry of intensities and complexities many times greater than the space circuits.

The law of the neuron is "All or None." The nerve cell is either on or off. Intensity and novelty determine how many synaptic connections and how many other circuits are turned on. Words and thoughts are clumsy and slow, learned laryngeal responses. To express neurological consciousness the human must learn multilevel, multisensory electronic means of communication and interperson linkage.

RAPTURE CIRCUIT

DURING THE LATTER 20ᵀᴴ CENTURY Western culture discovered the Rapture Circuit. Sexual liberation, sensual training, hedonic dress and grooming, massage, the eroticization of all forms of art define a cultural evolution. Current appraisals indicate that sensory pleasure and luxury constitute the biggest business in the West today.

Before our era, sixth circuit neuro-electric ecstasy existence had been known to many. Educated epileptics, courageous yogies—certainly Lao Tse, Heraclitus, and Vedantic sages, among others, had activated the "post-planetary" simultaneous complexity of the brain. But until the electronic efflorescence of the 1940s, when man's electronic dexterity made it possible to write the formulae for escaping gravity, no external language existed to describe neuro-electric ecstatic phenomena. Interstellar voyages require an understanding of Einsteinian-Lorentzian space-time

AUTO-MOBILE! JOY-RIDE YOUR BODY.

THE BODY IS THE CAR; THE NERVOUS SYSTEM IS THE DRIVER.

formulae. Neurologicians understand that increasing velocity dilates time and decreases aging, realize that off-planet exploration should be called "time travel." When we leave the planet, we leave place and enter time.

Up until now electronic instruments have been used for survival and for somatic-sensory rapture—television and FM radio. Sixth-circuit communication requires that we master and eroticize electronic computer-synthesizer technology.

Sixth-circuit neurological linkage is the "adolescence of time." This tuning-in phase of evolution will involve mastery of time-dilation and contraction, extraplanetary "time" travel, brain-computer linkage, person-person neural linkage—telepathy, routinized personal electronic communication and construction of new mini-worlds in High Orbit.

EXAMINING DEATH

DURING HIGH-DOSE LSD SESSIONS, subjects experience dying and report either personal sixth-circuit or genetic memories and forecasts. LSD has been administered to many dying patients because it seems to resign them to their forthcoming demise.

Neurogenetic theory predicts the discovery of an enzyme found within the nerve cells of dying animals. This chemical, synthesized and administered to healthy subjects under optimal voluntary conditions, will produce the experience of death with no effect on normal body function. We hypothesize that the "G-pill" will suspend space and body imprints and allow consciousness to tap the final dialogue between the DNA master code and the servant neuron. Then humankind will have an experimental tool for examining what happens when we die.

THE SEVENTH CIRCUIT
NEURO-GENETIC

THE THEME OF THE NEURO-GENIC CIRCUIT is "I am immortal" and is located anatomically within the neuron, mediating communication between the DNA nucleus of the cell and the neuron's memory-synthesizing structures. When the body faces a threat to life, alarm signals flash throughout the neural network. When these messages

WHEN WE LEAVE THE PLANET, WE LEAVE PLACE AND ENTER TIME TRAVEL.

indicate that death is imminent, the nervous system shuts off local hive imprints and abandons outlying sensory and somatic receiving centers. The neural "drop-out" begins.

STANDING OUTSIDE

AT THIS POINT, the nervous system operates at the sixth circuit of neuro-electric ecstasy. Ecstasy, which literally means "standing outside," comes to everyone at the moment of dying. A few have survived the brush of death and returned to report the acceleration, simultaneity, and intensity. "I was floating and could see my lifeless body." "My entire life flashed before my eyes."

In clock time, the neurological ecstasy of dying lasts no more than a few minutes, but subjectively, it is experienced as millions of years. When body time is disconnected—the nervous system is free to tune in to its own hundreds of millions of signals per second.

As the dying experience continues, the neural network itself begins to cut out. The energy required to fire signals across synaptic barriers weakens. Consciousness retreats to the neuron itself. The final dialogue is between the memory-synthesizing centers within the neuron and the DNA code in the cell nucleus. The last voice is the explanatory whisper of the genetic blueprint: "Here's where we came from. Here's where we're going."

SOUL

FOR THREE BILLION YEARS the DNA code has been building improved bodies to continue evolution sequence toward its goal: Increased intelligence. The DNA code is a miniaturized time-capsule of consciousness, the invisible essence—the wisdom of life. Most of the characteristics formerly attributed to the "soul" now describe the functions of DNA, whose complex message may originate from higher intelligences in other solar systems.

In the past, the seventh circuit was activated at the onset of awareness of the "death" process, when consciousness retracts from hive imprints, from the body, and from the neural circuit itself, to centers on meta-species signals from the DNA code. The discoveries of DNA structure and of powerful neurogenetic drugs like LSD and Ketamine allow controlled, precise, voluntary activation of the Seventh Circuit.

THE EIGHTH CIRCUIT
NEURO-QUANTUM

THE THEME OF THE NEURO-QUANTUM CIRCUIT is "We are spirit" and is concerned with metaphysiological, nuclear, and galactic time. Technological mastery alone will not let humans leave the planet and solar system. Our species will not be capable of high orbital colonization until DNA has been deciphered, until the neurogenetic circuit has been imprinted and integrated into the eighth-circuit network.

EVOLUTIONARY PERSPECTIVE

NEUROGENETIC PHILOSOPHY HOLDS that every living creature plays an evolutionary role as part of an evolutionary blueprint. Each human egg supply or sperm library carries thousands of unique mutant characteristics, many within the nervous system and morphologically undetectable. The evolutionary perspective sees humankind's goal as mutational, sees the individual as student, agent, and assistant in the evolutionary process.

To turn on and think like one's body is the first degree of time consciousness. To tune in and think like one's nervous system is the second degree. To drop out and think like one's DNA genetic code is the third degree of post-hive, post-planetary consciousness. According to the present theory, this access to the "silent hemisphere" is a natural evolutionary and maturational stage. Nature, extravagant in experiment, is always parsimonious in structural efficiency and would hardly design the brain so that half its neural potential remains unused.

When the four adult imprints are transcended, consciousness has access to areas of the nervous system ordinarily blocked off. Many schizoids are exceptionally original, visionary, prophetic, and creative. Throughout history, shamanic persons

THE DNA CODE IS A MINIA-TURIZED TIME-CAPSULE OF CONSCIOUSNESS.

have transcended hive-conditioned circuits. Since early imprinting stimuli are totally external, meditation and deliberate isolation make it possible to escape extra-survival dominance. Injesting certain entheogens suspend imprints and provide novel states of consciousness that, according to the present theory, should be accompanied by increased right-cortical activity as measured by EEG.

ACTIVATION PROBLEMS

A HIGH PERCENTAGE—perhaps half—of alienated humans are in trouble with their hives because their brains are operating in advanced "Neuro Realities" that are not yet conventionally acceptable. Four "schizoid" situations occur when neural circuits designed for post-terrestrial ecologies are activated prematurely.

First is acute hypersensitivity to sensory-somatic stimuli—the "fragile artist" syndrome. Second is telepathic, "psychic" neuro-electric sensitivities like Nikola Tesla. Third is genetic, interspecies, reincarnation-prereincarnation sensitivities like Luther Burbank, Dr. Jagadis Chandra Bose. Fourth is atomic-nuclear, quantum sensitivities.

When futique circuits are activated in unsympathetic environments, where the first four adult imprints are not self-confidently successful, the attendant sensitivities are usually painful and alienating. But neurological metamorphosis opens up the possibility of more advanced conditioning, designed for more complex consciousness and communication.

TO KEEP DEVELOPING YOU MUST KEEP FAITH IN YOUR TOUGHT, INNCENT POTENTIAL TO GROW.

CONSCIOUSNESS VACUUM

THE PLANET HAS NOW REACHED the halfway point between its birth swirl and its solar incandescence. The human species reached its neurological halfway point during World War II, the final convulsive exaggeration of fourth-circuit mental-manipulation behavior. A new generation was born with allegiance to their own nervous systems, rather than to national duty and hive moral-ity. Everyone born since Hiroshima, begining with the Baby Boomers, shares a conspira-torial knowledge that the old planetary way is over, that old dogmas are dead.

MEDITATION AND DELIBERATE ISOLATION MAKE IT POSSIBLE TO ESCAPE EXTRA-SUR-VIVAL DOMINANCE.

An enormous vacuum in consciousness exists today, greater than the philosophic anticipation that swept the Roman world years ago. Despite the heroics, the earth-bound phase of humanity was, let's face it, a dreary half-life. Every pre-WWII philosophy and religion is pessimistic about human destiny. Not one offers anything but an exhausted, virtuous peace of mind, excited only by the pleasures of militant conversion or persecution of the non-believer.

ESCAPE

ESCAPE! It's about time for the physical neurological linkage and the genetic fusion that define the higher love. We are ready for the future life that has rested dormant within our bodies. Our eyes touch, our seed fuses. There is nothing to fear, your eyes see behind me—no reason to struggle. What is above is as below—no shame. Your right hand guides my left—no guilt. We combine every sexual-social possibility. We are beautiful.

CHAPTER 4

MiGRATioN

S O THE TIME IS RIPE FOR EXO-PSYCHOLOGY. Exo-
Psychology spins off from the exobiology concept
made respectable by Carl Sagan. Exobiology studies
the existence of life off the surface of our embryo
planet. Panspermia was given credibility by Crick,
Orgel, Hoyle, and Wickramasinghe. Platoons of
sober Soviet scientists solemnly weighed and assayed
cosmonauts. For a time there were multimillion
dollar budgets for space medicine.

Studies of post-terrestrial human psychology have
been executed by Air Force scientists since World
War II. One four-volume epic published in the late
1940s studied the effects of Allied bombing on
Germany, which included accounts of the stresses
and blisses of high-altitude flight, the psychoneural
selection, testing, and training of astronauts. Was
the irritable rebellion of the second Skylab crew
premonition of later revolts of Space Colonists
against home-base controls?

Such NASA and Pentagon researches, while
grandly-funded, were seen as exotic specialties far

removed from mainstream psychology which had become a most profitable sort of "auto" repair, with unimaginative technicians patching up domesticated primates and restoring them to useful efficiency. A bang-out-the-dents-personality-renovation may be exciting to the limping owner of the obsolescent genetic vehicle, but the scientfic aspects of psychology are clearly being absorbed by sociobiology and neurogenetics.

PSYCHOLOGISTS AS ROLE MODELS

INFLUENTIAL MEMBERS of the cultural establishment are expected to be paragons of the values they seek to implement. Thus today's psychologists tend to be highly overconditioned, industrious, conventionally virtuous, and domesticated.

THE GOAL OF 20TH CENTURY PSYCHOLOGY WAS TO PATCH UP DOMESTICATED PRIMATES.

As prime conditioner of fellow humans, we psychologists and educators are expected to be exemplars—calm, serious, controlled, sensibly cynical, smugly pessimistic, and above all, rational. We are expected to understand the Master Plan and to help our charges to understand it. To study the unconditioned state, to produce pleasure in subjects, and to act in a natural, hedonic manner would lead to excommunication. Fortunately, psychologists' role will evolve, however. The psychologist of the future will be master ecstacist. S/he will be identified by hir radiant vibrations. After all, s/he has years of graduate training in making people feel good.

REPRESSION OF FUN

ORPHEUS, early prophet of the pleasure principle, was torn to bits by enraged middle-aged women. Dionysus never received tenure. The alchemists along with their deconditioning drugs—elivir vitae— were driven underground. Hypnosis is a classic technique for temporarily altering conditioning, so no surprise that Mesmer was anathernized.

Reich, whose genius is just beginning to be recognized, died in federal prison. The essence of his teaching is that neurosis, psychosis, totalitarianism, and other social pathologies are the result of conditioned restriction of sexual pleasure. His prescription for a happy, free society: Help people make love longer and better. Kick out the jams.

PSYCHOLOGY OF MIGRATION

SUBJECTS OF FUTURE PSYCHOLOGICAL STUDY will surely include the movement of gene-pools according to predictable patterns of swarming. The evolution of new social-genetic forms. Understanding of genetic castes. Human leucocyte antigen research. Histocompatibility (blood-type-studies) opening up the Pandora's treasure chest of neurocompatibility, DNA compatibility, cloning. How about recombinant DNA technicians splicing in a "jolly" gene to replace a "mean" gene?

But advances in our understanding and rearrangement of human nature are meaningless as long as our species remain trapped on a

SWARMING PATTERNS ARE PREDICTABLE.

shrinking planet with mammalian territorial pressure reaching the explosion point.

Exo-Psychology's immediate, practical survival aspect is the psychology of migration. Questions for study include: Who gets to colonize space? What are the genetic predispositions and neuro-aptitudes of the successful frontiersperson?

Movement from water to land activated an enormous explosion of new species. Migration from the landlocked, one-G planet can be expected to produce a similar eruption as we are transformed from barnacles to high-flying, fast-moving neuroelectroids. (It is of haunting evolutionary interest to recall that the monumental research on barnacles was published, in 1840, by Charles Darwin.) Those who leave the sessile, sedentary stage of planetary life to become high-orbital habitats will have to exhibit paradoxical polarities, extraordinary individualism and self-confidence combined with extraordinary abilities to work with and rely on others.

STAGES OF MIGRATION

THE FIRST WAVES OF MIGRANTS usually represent extremes of individualism. Following waves tend to be the more traditional culture. But in space migration, the real kicker comes from those who will be born in high orbit. Second-generation migrants who spend their entire lives in multiple gravity looking down—out—at the small, blue, spinning Old World. New neuromuscular and neuro-endocrine solutions will characterize these ad-vanced futants.

THE FIRST WAVES OF MIGRANTS REPRESENT EXTREMES OF INDIVIDUALISM.

We are not terrestrials designed to spend our lives pasted to the surface of a sphere terraformed by someone else. We must focus on neuro-logic brain know-how, serial imprinting. Learn to use your head. Satire and affectionate ridicule is the basic key of evolution. "Really, Leo, isn't it ludicrous to run around on four feet when you can climb on two?"

Thus I admit that I have heaped some scorn on Pavlovian-Skinnerian methods of behavior change that lead to insectoid-urbanold fourth-circuit realities, and I have mocked the fifth-circuit hippie-somatic, back-to-body-naturism.

ATTENTION: DNA has recalled the 1966 Hippy Model to repair structural defects, including a tendency to disregard navigational intelligence at high altitudes and failures in transmission from mechanical-muscular to neuro-electric intelligence.

YOU CAN MOVE INTO THE FUTURE ONLY AS FAR AS YOU HAVE SUCCESSFULLY MASTERED THE PAST.

CHAPTER 5

NAVIGATIONAL CRISIS

THE CAUSE OF THE SUFFERING AND SCARCITY that threatens humanity is neuro-political. The current malaise of the affluent nations demonstrates clearly that material rewards are not enough. The crisis the human race now faces is best described as navigational. Humanity has lost the map, the compass, the guidebook; they have misplaced the genetic code.

Life on Earth, through the instrumentality of the human nervous system, has begun to establish colonies in space, from whence it can more accessibly contact life in the galaxy. In our cells, we know that we, who are about to leave this small satellite of a peripheral star, are neither alone nor unique. Our most important challenge is to prepare ourselves neurologically to meet the "relatives" with whom we share the galaxy.

Some will protest that human intelligence and resources should be used to solve agonizing terrestrial problems of unequal distribution. These protests, however sincere, are historically wrong and genetically futile.

LAW OF LEAST EFFORT

MEN AND WOMEN WHO KNOW where they're going, who share a vision beyond the local-mundane, will learn quickly, work effectively, grow naturally, socialize lovingly, and evolve gracefully because of the genetic Law of Least Effort. Both species and individuals coast along on serene stupidity until faced with evolutionary challenges, at which point both species and individuals become smarter, very much faster. WW II provides an interesting illustration. Basic principles of atomic structure, rocket propulsion, and radar had been well-known for decades. But under pressure of the Technological Imperative, the American and German scientific communities got smart—fast

THE MIGRATION SOLUTION

MIGRATION IS NATURE'S CLASSIC SOLUTION to overpopulation, scarcity, and competition. When humanity begins to work for extraterrestrial migration, the competition for material acquisition will gradually diminish because unlimited space, energy, and resources await in the solar system.

This simple-minded perspective of biological evolution presents hundreds of neogenetic ideas for which the human species is now ready. The reader should expect, therefore, that hir conditioned symbol-system is going to be jolted with unexpected, novel symbol combinations. A 21st Century human would find it most difficult to explain "now" to an average fellow from the 18th Century. Some goodwill and openness is necessary in interspecies dia-

HUMANITY HAS LOST THE MAP, THE COMPASS, THE GUIDEBOOK; THEY HAVE MISPLACED THE GENETIC CODE.

LEARN TO USE YOUR HEAD. logues of this sort. This is exactly the situation that will exist when Higher Intelligence begins to communicate with human space colonies. Is there anything more interesting or vital thing to do than to create the future?

EVOLUTON OF THE NERVOUS SYSTEM

THE PERSON WHO CAN DIAL AND TUNE THE CIRCUITS of the nervous system is not just more intelligent, but can be said to operate at a higher, more complex level of evolution. A powerful instrument for conscious evolution, the nervous system can be understood and employed for genetic tasks.

Emotional, mental, sexual, and ethical behavior is based on accidental imprinting of the nervous system during "critical" or "sensitive" periods of development—a fact devastating to pretensions of free will and conscious choice. An impressive convergence of evidence suggests that the brain is a bio-chemical-electric computer in which each nerve impulse acts as an information "quantra" or "bit". The human being, at this stage of evolution, is a biological robot—automatically responding to genetic-template and childhood imprinting.

We can evaluate ourselves only in terms of the symbols our nervous systems have created. An anthropological report about *Homo sapiens* written by extraterrestrials from a more advanced civilization would conclude that intelligent life has not yet evolved on this planet. Other sciences have significance for future human destiny.

WHEN FACED WITH EVOLUTIONARY CHALLENGES WE BECOME SMARTER, FASTER.

ASTRONAUTICS

THE SIGNIFICANCE OF EXTRATERRESTRIAL FLIGHT has not yet been fully understood. Just as land-dwelling organisms rapidly develop neural and physiological equipment for the new environment, this transition to zero-gravity and extraterrestrial radiation will trigger off genetic and neurological changes necessary to adapt to interstellar life. The beginnings of exo-psychological adaptation can be noted in several lunar veterans who returned claiming cosmic insights (Mitchell), sophic revelations (Schweickart), and rebirth symptoms (Aldrin).

Astrophysics has determined that perhaps as many as half of the 100 billion stars in our local galaxy are older than our sun. Astronomers have discovered basic life molecules in outer space and in other star systems, making it highly probable that more advanced forms of intelligent life are around the neighborhood. So far, humans have been neurologically incapable of conceiving of higher intelligence.

The left-cortical mind, seat of the third-circuit mental-manipulation, naturally assumes that life from other solar systems will be hostile and competitive: galactic cowboys and Indians. Very few science fiction writers—Stapledon, Asimov, Clarke—specify the manifestations of superior species, except as bizarre extrapolations and extremes of current human culture.

CREATE CHANGE

WHATEVER THE MIND CAN CONCEIVE, it tends to create. As soon as humans accept the notion of as-yet-unactivated circuits in the nervous system, a new philosophy of an evolving nervous system will emerge—human nature seen from the vantage point of older species.

CHAPTER 6

NEUROGENETICS

NEUROGENETICS IS A NEW SCIENCE which studies the psychology, i.e., consciousness and behavior, of DNA-RNA. We assume that DNA contelligence is not restricted to planet Earth, but, indeed, was probably designed to return to extraterrestrial intelligence. Blueprints are remarkably similar from species to species. The DNA code can now be seen as a temporal blueprint unfolding sequentially like a tape-spool, transmitting preprogrammed construction plans from infancy, through childhood, adolescence, maturity, menopause, aging, and death. Individual ontology recapitulates species phylogeny—that the human embryo, for example, repeats the evolutionary cycle.

The theory of serial imprinting suggests that psychology repeats the evolutionary sequence: The baby recapitulates an invertebrate reality, the crawling child a mammalian reality, the preschool child a Paleolithic reality, the adolescent a domesticated-civilized reality.

SERIAL IMPRINTING REPEATS THE EVOLUTIONARY SEQUENCE.

FUTURE BLUEPRINTS

GENETICISTS ARE DISCOVERING "UNUSED" SECTIONS of the DNA, masked by histories and activated by proteins, which are thought to contain the blueprint of the future. Neurochemistry has discovered that neurotransmitter chemicals facilitate/inhibit nerve impulses and synaptic connections determining consciousness, emotion, memory, learning, and behavior. At the same time, psychopharmacology has discovered botanical and synthetic psychoactive agents that facilitate and inhibit states of consciousness and accelerate or dampen mental function.

The histone-masked sections of the DNA code can be studied to determine the sequence of future evolution. Just as the DNA code, in the nucleus of the cell, is the genetic brain, the nucleus of the atom is the elemental "brain" that designs and constructs atoms and molecules according to quantum logic. Physicist John Archibald Wheeler's work suggests that the atomic nucleus can receive, remember, integrate, and transmit information at extremely high velocities and can probably engage in most of the basic social behavior that we observe in living organisms.

TWO-WAY DNA DIALOGUE

WE INEVITABLY "PSYCHOLOGIZE" NATURE and personalize atomic events. Our minds cannot conceive of what we have never experienced. But psychological systems based on Newtonian geocentric principles have done little to harmonize human philosophy. Does it seem too fanciful to base psychological concepts on the laws and structures of physics, chemistry, and astronomy?

Our dialogue with DNA and our conversations with atomic-subatomic and astronomical energy signals must, however, be two-way. We must open our "minds" to receive the signals being sent to our nervous systems by DNA and by elemental intelligences. Since DNA creates us, it is logical, diplomatic, and theologically conventional to base our psychology upon molecular laws and designs, upon the laws and structures of nuclear physics and astronomy; to think of ourselves as "atoms" or even "stars"—radiating, decaying, attracting, repelling, receiving and transmitting, forming molecular social structures and possessing a characteristic electromagnetic personality.

NEURAL CHAUVINISM

FROM THE SCIENTIFIC VIEWPOINT, reality is an ocean of electromagnetic vibrations whirling momentarily into temporary structures—including bodies with nervous systems. Human consciousness—our personal reality—is determined by the point along the frequency spectrum where the neural dials are tuned. Our realities are defined by chunks of local environment attached to the nervous system at the time of imprinting.

Seasonal variations in solar radiation may alter DNA templating at the time of conception, determining human neurogenetic "types." The twelve Zodiac "signs" may crudely personalize twelve subspecies very different in neurological wiring, which reflect and recapitulate twelve stages of phylogenetic and human evolution. Each Zodiac "species" thus represents the mastery of one of the twelve neurological stages of evolution. As an aside, the tradition of using twelve peers in a trial by jury may be an unconscious recognition of the twelve subspecies populating human society.

MIMICKING INSECTS

JUST AS THE MEMBERS OF INSECT COLONIES are programmed to play certain roles necessary for hive survival—worker, drone, brood queen—so each of the twelve types of human species can be considered genetically separate. Each contributes to the evolutionary process and carries a printed-out nervous system geared to a specialized survival task. In addition, environment models imprinted during individual development define island realities such as language and dialects that vary from person to person and from group to group.

This unique specificity of reality means, among other things, that numerous cultural-imprint groups wander around the planet, for the most part in different realities. People unconsciously recognize this. Social avoidance and clustering tend to respond to these reality chauvinisms. The hive cannot tolerate other realities—anyone different is crazy or alien. But despite their neural machinery, humans communicate with each other about material needs with amazing efficiency.

HUMANS ARE NEUROLOGICALLY INCAPABLE
OF COCEIVING OF HIGHER INTELLIGENCE LIKE
THE CATERPILLAR THAT CAN'T CONCEIVE
BEING A BUTTERFLY.

MIGRATION IS NATURE'S SOLUTION
TO OVERPOPULATION, SCAR-
CITY, AND COMPETITION.

CHAPTER 7

¡MPRiNTiN9

THE NEWBORN BABY IS EQUIPPED with behavior patterns necessary for immediate survival. To turn towards the mothering stimulus and suckle. Shortly after birth, the baby's nervous system focuses all the sensory equipment on the soft, warm, milk-producing stimulus, and permanently photographs this picture as "survivally good" and safe. If this viscerotonic imprint is not taken because of absence of appropriate stimulus during the critical period, the basic "survival security" system is not effectively wired up to human contacts.

The infant body is like a spaceship floating on a strange new planet. The imprint is a neuro-umbilical lifeline extended from the nervous system, blindly groping for hospitable survival stimuli to which it attaches and roots, thus creating the reality island. Once attached, the nervous system is hooked for life—unless retracted by accidental trauma, or deliberately.

WE MUST OPEN OUR "MINDS" TO RECEIVE THE SIGNALS BEING SENT TO OUR NERVOUS SYSTEMS.

SEXUAL IMPRINTING

EACH OF THE FOUR NEURO-UMBILICAL LIFELINES is extended in turn when each neural circuit emerges. During adolescence, for example, there is a critical or "sensitive" period of sexual imprinting. The sexual antennae, heretofore rudimentary, emerge and blindly scan for a place to root.

The first time the sexual system is fired in all-out response, an imprint is taken, determining the sensory, emotional, mental, and social stimuli that facilitate subsequent arousal and discharge. Accidental vicissitudes of fourth-circuit sexual imprinting—early erections and orgasms—can create kinky fetishes well-known to psychiatrists.

SYMBOLIC IMPRINTING

THE NEUROLOGIC MECHANICS of the mental-symbolic third-circuit imprint are less familiar. The acquisition of speech and manipulative behavior is accomplished by moving the nine muscles of the larynx. When the child is mastering speech, the mental and emotional style of contiguous parents and, more important, older children determine whether the child's mind is open and trusting or withdrawn and rejecting. Once the child wires up a specific method of thinking, subsequent education has little effect on intellectual manipulation.

> **First Circuit Biosurvival Language:** Movements, sounds, and behaviors that express security, pain, or physical threat. Eating, vomiting, sucking, disgust, embracing, moaning, physically aggressing or menacing.

> **Second Circuit Emotional Language:** Gestures, postures, and verbal tones that communicate a status message. Gestural signals for affiliation, dominance, submission, begging, giving, coercion, and passive complaint require no cross-cultural dictionary.

Each culture has a specific status vocabulary of accents, gestures, ornaments, conspicuous possessions, postures. In the suburbs, a Cadillac indicates highest status; in the slums, a Cadillac indicates a pimp or cocaine dealer. And so it goes.

REALITY GULFS

EACH OF US DEALS WITH A WORLD DEFINED by a unique pattern of neural wires and fixed umbilical lifelines. We try to understand emerging stages of human development by analogy to the metamorphosis of insects, since we are too close to the situation to appreciate metamorphosis in ourselves. Just so, we can understand the uniqueness of electro-neural "reality" by considering the consciousness islands of other species. We see a mouse run across the floor and a snake turn its head and strike. We assume that the snake "sees" what we see—a furry, brown animal. However, the snake uses heat receptors to locate prey. Programmed to strike at heat, the snake senses a neon spot of "warm" moving across its screen.

Human beings often interact across similar "reality" gulfs. Robot-programmed as differently as the snake, we vary in the number of languages we can exchange. The most primitive humans communicate and manipulate only in

ANYONE DIFFERENT IS CRAZY OR ALIEN.

the oral dialect of their childhood village. The
highly civilized counterparts have mastered hundreds
of symbol systems, can speak
and write each other in several
languages, cooperatively manipulate a wide variety of mechanical
artifacts, professional sequences, scientific codes,
sports and game rituals.

EVERY BODY HAS A FAVORITE REALITY.

In communicating with another person, nonverbal cues establish that first-circuit is safe and second-circuit is cooperative. The next step is to establish which muscle-thought languages are shared and
can be appropriately exchanged. Most human inter-
actions—buying, selling, superficial socializing—are
brief and limited. Extended conversations are loaded
with complexity because emotional factors inevitably
intrude. Giving information to others is often
resented because information possession implies
power.

The mental-symbolic third-circuit is activated
when the young child is in a position of weakness.
Adults or superiors teach the child symbol systems.
The ability to learn symbols is determined by
emotional context—the person with the information
is placed in a superior position over the receiver.
Just as chemicals "fix" a photographic image on
film, so is the neural image of the island-reality
"fixed" by synaptic chemical bonds at the time of
imprinting.

ILLUSION OF REALITY

A CHILD GROWING UP FINDS A CERTAIN STABILITY and
consistency in the social cues s/he imprints. Hir
parents speak the same language, share rituals with
the family next door. This consensual agreement

provides the illusion of a "reality" shared with those in hir culture group. "Sanity" is defined in terms of one's ability to convince oneself that s/he perceives what others do. Social psychologists' cognitive dissonance experiments show how easily and naturally humans distort objective data to fit neural expectations.

We believe what we are imprinted to believe. We think that the tiny turf to which our neuro-umbilical lifelines attach is "reality." The fact of separate, subjective realities based on individual imprints is frightening for the preneurological human. Recall the parable of the blind men and the elephant? This separateness accounts for the terror felt in the presence of an "insane" person—who, in many cases, is actually aware of the neural insulation separating people and might be considered more sane and accurate than the deluded "normals." Casteneda's Don Juan in *Tales of Power* gives a good description of the imprint reality.

> Sorcerers say that we are inside a bubble into which we are placed at the moment of birth.... It begins to close until it has sealed us in. That bubble is our perception. We live inside that bubble all of our lives... until all our attention is caught by it and the description becomes a view.

FEAR TRIGGERS IMPRINTING

THE FIRST-CIRCUIT BIO-EMERGENCY SYSTEM commands millions of survival actions. Early "danger" imprints and genetic programs cue this powerful, basic system, which, mobilized, affects every organ in the body. The intransigence of human phobias and security blankets is caused by chemico-electric synaptic patterns.

Security means that imprinted lifelines are securely fastened to a stable island-reality. When action inside the body becomes so intense as to alter synapse chemistry, imprint lifelines to the external environment are retracted. Shock, illness, trauma, drugs, child delivery, stimulus deprivation, and electrical charge.

WE BELIEVE WHAT WE ARE IMPRINTED TO BELIEVE.

The result is a new reality for the patient. When the somatic infection is cured, the emergency "sick" wiring may remain in operation, preventing the restoration of normal function. Conversely, infection or malfunction may require curative changes blocked by the normal "wiring." This may help explain accupuncture. The needles have little effect on the fleshy system, but—particularly when energized with mild electric charges—may affect the synaptic programs.

IMMEDIATE LEARNING

THE NOTION OF IMPRINTING as a form of immediate and irreversible "learning" has created some confusion, since according to the classic definitions of most psychological theories, "Learning occurs as the result of practice." But psychological theories of learning based on observations of external, visible behavior pay little attention to the internal, invisible neurological situation. First, the imprint hooks the natural unconditioned response to an external stimulus—the releaser mechanism. Conditioning then connects—wires up neurally—other stimuli with the imprinted stimuli. Learned stimuli can then trigger the response imprinted to the original stimulus. If the infant's first-circuit biosurvival mechanisms are positively imprinted to Mother, other learned cues such as her aprons, kitchen, perfume, can also trigger off the "positive-approach" response.

NOT CONDITIONING

SKINNERIANS ATTEMPT to "shape" symbolic third-circuit behavior is a futile, coercive business. Operant conditioning "works" by means of immediate and reoccuring reinforcement.

CONDITIONING BIOCHEMICALLY LINKS A NEW STIMULUS WITH AN IMPRINT.

I recall an enthusiastic Skinnerian researcher who reported to the Center for Personality Research at Harvard on the applications of operant conditioning to patients in a mental hospital. The behavior to be inhibited was "hallucinatory talk." Now many among us believe that hallucinations have a functional role in the psyche. Automatically extinguishing hallucinations might restrict some message of importance, even if not understood or considered useful to the psychologist's reality. Using immediate reinforcement, he produced a cigarette every time the patient made a non-hallucinatory comment and took the cigarette away every time the patient hallucinated. He gleefully announced that the rate of hallucinatory comments dropped by a significant level.

Even more impressive changes in behavior accompanied the giving or deprivation of food. The young researcher glumly complained that hospital rules prevented them from carrying out his experiment to the point of starvation: "If we had total control over food intake, we could really shape behavior." The operant conditioner may not have heard the comment by one staff member that most of the dictators in world history had used this technique.

CONDITIONING CANNOT CHANGE AN IMPRINTED REALITY

IMPOSING PERSONAL VALUES

A MORE ENLIGHTENED BEHAVIORIST, as they became known, pointed out that the choice "extinguishing hallucinatory comments" as a treatment objective has more to do with the researcher's own values—domestication is good—than with operant conditioning principles discovered by B.F. Skinner. The resulting "improved" patient may well still hallucinate but has "learned" to not comment on it. Operant conditioning principles work equally well on "internal behavior" as on external visible behavior. In this view, hallucinating is an internal behavior. The question is: Should hallucinations be extinguished? Most psychologists—Skinnerian and touchy-feely both—say, "Yes!"

Keep in mind that psychologists, psychiatrists and, most of all, social workers are the mind police. To be so, their minds are well-policed! Unleashed from the hive mentaility, psychologist such as myself are among the most dangerous people. We are rennagades, pider-pipers, and tricksters challenging hive-order and beaconing you to migrate. Do you have any wonder that I was persecuted for my ideas?

While the researcher lamented that he couldn't withhold food to effect behavior change, training obedience with food is commonplace. How do we train dogs? All parents use food to extract obedience. "Go to your room without dinner, young man!" And parents are even more skilled in the use of attention! No one is free of this powerful conditioning experience. Seeking acceptance and avoiding rejection are at the heart of peer pressure and hive conformity.

IMPRINTING RULES

TWO GROUPS OF TECHNOCRATS clamor to change the behavior of their fellow citizens: Right-wing punitive coercers, and left-wing liberal rewarders. Punitive coercion works only as long as the threat remains, and thus requires a police state. Liberal social psychologists believe that they can change behavior by supportive, egalitarian methods—head-start programs, Peace Corps, busing, tutoring. Both groups' attempts are futile because they attempt to recondition, rather than reimprint.

The more intelligent experimental psychologists, for whom Skinner is spokesman, believe they can impose behavior change by involuntary operant conditioning. This, however, works only when the conditioners are continually present to reinforce. Left to their own devices, the "subjects" immediately drift back to the magnetism of the imprint and genetic template.

But we are not left to our own devices. There is the "program"—the words running through our minds, what psychologists call "self-talk" and Buddhist call "the chatter." With this internal monolog we continue to reinforce our programming with the images and words in our minds—the programs that run our biocomputer. We perpetuate our conditioning. Absence of a negative consequence is experienced as a "reward" and functions to reinforce the conditioning or program. When we think about the possibility of a negative event, which may be so habitual that we no longer listen to our mind's chatter, and when the negative event doesn't

IMPRINTS CAN ONLY BE CHANGED BIOCHEMICALLY.

actually happen, we experience a subtle relief. "Ah, it's okay. Phew!" This relief from the absence of a dreaded event, such as rejection, punishment, pain, etc., reinforces and continues the conditioned program.

Imprinting, on the other hand, requires no reinforcement. Let me imprint the infant, and you try to condition the child; let me imprint the child, and you try to condition the adolescent. The imprint requires no repeated reward or punishment; the neural fix is permanent. Conditioned associations, on the contrary, wane and disappear with lack of repetition.

CONDITIONED RESPONSES CAN BE UNLEARNED, WHILE WITH IMPRINTING THE NEURAL FIX IS PERMANENT.

In order to condition human behavior, get control of stimuli early in childhood and maintain this control throughout life. In the psychological utopia, continual psychological testing would identify potential troublemakers early in the game and special conditioning programs would eliminate individual eccentricity.

CONTROL AND SECRECY

THE CASE FOR THE POLITICAL CONDITIONERS can be simply paraphrased. To make human beings dutiful, virtuous, reliable, prompt, efficient, happy, law-abiding, government psychologists must have total control over the citizenry and there must be total secrecy and censorship. They must be mind police

One dissident, one freedom-oriented psychologist can totally disrupt psychological fascism by public exposure. If parents and children are warned about the method of conditioning, they can consciously decide whether to resist, passively or actively. Most psychological tests are ineffective if the subject has been warned about their purpose and construction. Even brainwashing drugs can be counteracted by the person who learns the specific effects of neurochernicals.

Fun speaks to the power of conscious self-talk, of deliberately changing the words of the program operating the robot's biocomputer. We can use conditioning principles to program ourselves as we choose—at least in theory. Ideas and awakenings can lead us to taking charge. One dissident, freedom-pushing psychologist's ideas can be disruptive. Rock groups, such as the *Grateful Dead,* served the same function and are equally disliked by Big Brother.

TURN ON AND THINK LIKE YOUR BODY; TUNE IN AND THINK LIKE YOUR NERVOUS SYSTEM; DROP OUT AND THINK LIKE YOUR DNA GENETIC CODE.

CHAPTER 8

DOMESTiCATE

oR MUTATE

HUMANITY NOW FACES A GENETIC CROSSROAD. Some will choose to solidify social conditioning by manipulating the child's environment and thus domesticating the imprint. We get Maoism. Others will choose to mutate to a higher level where each person is taught to manage and control hir own imprinting and conditioning. We can expect that many different social groups will emerge along each direction.

RECONDITIONING IMPRINTS

AFTER EACH DAILY TIDE of association and reward-punishment, coercive behavior-control methods must be repeated. The coercive nature of learned behavior appears voluntary; in fact, the conditioned robot is obsessively drawn back to hir place in the sandbox. If we remove the symbol-rewarding environment or fail to produce the conditioned stimulus, the humanoid robot goes mad, because s/he has nothing to do.

IMPRINTING LIMITS REALITY TO THE LOCAL ENVIRONMENT.

We can accurately speak of stimulus junkies. Social deprivation creates desperate reward-hunger. The social reality of conditioned response requires continual rewarding. The ordeal of Sisyphus was an exciting adventure compared to the monotony of social conditioning. Trying to recondition an imprint with reward-punishment is like dropping single grains of sand on a steel pattern. Decades of sand can wear down the imprint. The aging politician gets lazy, the aging ladies man becomes too fatigued to seduce.

REPRINTING WITH LSD

To change the shape of metal forms, one must apply enough energy to rearrange the molecules. So with neural imprint. Massive biochemical energy is necessary to loosen the molecular synaptic bonds. With the present repertoire neuro-electric Sixth-circuit neurotransmitter drugs, it is apparently possible to reimprint only about once a week. It takes from 5 to 7 days for the reimprinted nervous system to harden into new circuits. Ill-prepared LSD sessions tend to reimprint the past conditioned structure, thus charging with new energy the habit patterns of the old island reality. People who have taken LSD often complain that, after a while, the "trips" are the same. If the recasting of the mind occurs over and over again in the same place with the same set of characters, this is like having the most precise and expensive photographic equipment and, without moving it, continuing to photograph the same object.

IMPRINTING FIX

1HE IMPRINT-FIX IS SUDDEN. Post-imprint conditioning, centering on the positive and negative poles of the imprint, takes time and repetition. Around the initial imprint, billions of conditioned associations build up over the years, forming the structure of personality. Where new models are imprinted, it takes time to start building up new circles of conditioned reflexes. Some early researchers concluded that a six-month wait should occur between LSD sessions to "work through the new insights." The exo-psychological phrase is "to allow new conditioning to network around the new imprints."

Reimprinting sessions, therefore, require careful planning so that previous aspects of realities that one wishes to exist in future reality are present to be imprinted, and that during the "sensitive" period, new models remain around to allow new associations to build up around them.

"SEE" THE WORLD

MOST WORLD TRAVELERS move their robot-bodies from country to country, experiencing only symbolic versions of home. Two neurologicians, a newly married couple, embarked on a psychedelic world tour. Their procedure was to fly to a country and inquire as to the "spiritual" center of that nation. In India, they were told to go to Benares. In Greece, to Eleusis; in Japan to Kyoto. Then in Kyoto, they asked where the spiritual center, the "soul" of Kyoto, was to be found. They spent a week reading about the history, politics, culture, art, myths of Japan and Kyoto, then went to the "holiest" place, ingested LSD—a sixth-circuit neuroactive chemical—that opened the nervous system to new imprints, which in this case were structured by the architecture and regalia of the Emperor's palace. For six hours they absorbed the signals of the place and became neurologically "Japanesed."

This is the way to "see the world"—to retract imprint roots and move the unattached nervous system to a new locale. Without such flexible vulnerability, we can experience nothing outside the membrane formed at adolescence or, in the case of women, their last childbirth. Such neural touring is no end in itself, but a rudimentary training exercise for the brain's serial possibilities. The neurological goal is to increase consciousness and intelligence. But when the nervous system can move and change realities by serial reimprinting, its own limitations become apparent; basic genetic dimensions of reality-construction are limited and guided by the genetic template. This most powerful determinant of human behavior cannot

HUMAN BEINGS INTERACT ACROSS "REALITY" GULFS.

be changed, only understood and adapted until post-larval humanity has evolved genetic engineering.

IMPRINT DNA CODE

THE MOST INTELLIGENT USE of the nervous system is to imprint the DNA code. The evolution of humanity of billions of years to come may already be preprogrammed in the genetic code, blocked from expression by chemical barriers called "histories." The blueprint of DNA has designed us to move life off the planet and eventually evolve beyond matter as we now know it. It is about time to use our heads to become very contelligent, very rapidly.

One who allows hirself to be controlled by conditioning or imprinting is accepting robothood. It is of little use, however, to go on reimprinting earthbound human or somatic realities. The neuro-electric sixth-circuit is designed for extraterrestrial existence, for genetic consciousness. Neurotransmitter drugs are thus seen to be post-adult in function.

IT IS TIME TO USE OUR HEADS TO BECOME VERY
CONTELLIGENT, VERY RAPIDLY.

CHAPTER 9

FUTURE SHOCK

U NTIL NOW, human beings have been neurologically unable to conceive of the future. This inhibition—neophobia—is genetic. For the caterpillar to "think" about flying would be survivally risky. Earth time involves short periods and narrow perspectives. The farmer looks to the next harvest, the politician to the next election, parents to their children.

The four-brained person does not want to know about the future because it threatens the stability of the reality imprint. There is a taboo about future forecast. *Future Shock* by Alvin Toffler describes the terror and confusion created by a world different from one's childhood realities. Even scientific groups are curiously unable to foresee evolving neurological-mutational change. The Club of Rome, the RAND Corporation Think Tank, and Herman Kahn all extrapolate material trends of the past. Thus are we told that the future will be a global extension of a Swedish Los Angeles. Most current "futurists" forecast an air-conditioned ant hill world in which personal freedom and creativity are limited by population, scarcity, and restrictive social control.

TOO EARLY TO MIGRATE

THE 1960s WITNESSED A WIDESPREAD RETRACTION of standard adult imprints. The new "hippie" imprints were not thoughtfully selected. They were a "drop-out" away from the parent-culture and an unfortunate tendency to reject technology and scientific thinking. The drug culture of the 1960s wandered around, "spaced out" and "high," but with no place to go. They were too early for interstellar migration. Into this neural vacuum rushed the karma dealers, Jesus salesmen, and spiritualists providing occult terms and other-worldly explanations for the new transcendental states. After retracting imprints from the material culture, the 1960s went back to Jesus, Hasidism, India, the nature simplicity of the pioneers—the consciousness fads became soothing terrestrial "turn-offs," offering peace of mind for premature mutants. The waterbed, with its hint of zero-gravity sensory freedom, is an example of a neuro-somatic fifth-circuit fad, for example.

HOW MUCH FUTURE CAN YOU HARNESS INTO YOUR LIFE RIGHT NOW?

RATE OF EVOLUTION

IT IS NATURAL THAT THE FIRST GENERATION to mutate would appear confused, disoriented, frivolous, irritatingly vague. A mutation always disturbs the core culture. No one wants the reality game to become bigger than one's childhood imprints. But the genetic timetable schedules mutations with relentless continuity. And the rate of evolution is accelerating. Physique, neurological function, ecology, density and diversity of population are changing at an accelerated rate. Consider the human situation 100 years ago. Now assume that the same rate of accelerated change continues. How will we evolve in the next 1,000 years?

Evolution produces an increasing spectrum of differentiations. About seventy-five million years ago, certain insectivore lemurs contained the seed-source from which 193 varieties of primates, including us humans, were to emerge. Of the next 100 persons you meet, probably each will evolve into a new species different from you as the rabbit from the giraffe.

GENETIC FUTIQUE

THE WORK OF BRUCE NIKLAS at Duke University reminds us of the intransigence of chromosomal patterns. If chromosome strands are experimentally disarrayed by poking them with a micro-needle, the molecules move back into the original sequence—much the way iron filings "swim" into position in response to magnetism. This suggests that some sort of energy-field pattern operates to keep the DNA code coherent and logical. The work of geneticists like Paul, Stein, and Kleinsmith suggests that histories mask the half of the DNA code containing the futique design of the organism. The error of genetic democracy led Gauguin to ask, "Where did we come from and where are we going?" Each of us transmits a very different precoded design. The question can only be asked, "Where am I going? What genetic futique do I carry in my genes?"

PRE-MUTANT RESISTANCE

EXO-PSYCHOLOGY HOLDS THAT HUMANS EXISTS in a reality defined by four survival imprints. Although the brain receives one hundred million impulses a second, mundane consciousness is limited to the four imprinted gameboards. The unevolved human has no interest in you unless your behavior offers meaning in terms of hir limited reality-island. They do not like to receive information unless it immediately rewards their emotional status.

Unevolved humans submit themselves only to new symbols that build on established systems or give promise of future rewards. This resistance to learning is neurological and biochemical. New ideas require a change in the wiring and literally cause a "headache." That unevolving humans learn almost no new symbol systems after childhood explains why it takes at least one generation for a new idea to be understood.

Few symbols now exist for post-larval "butterfly" processes. Similarly communicating with unevolved humans or "larvals" about sexual, philosophic, or ethical matters enters dangerous terrain.

When sensed as different, sexual-social fourth-circuit moral and social symbols and behaviors trigger responses of passion, even violence. Because of this sensitivity, humans tend to avoid philosophic discussions about life, death, philosophic ultimates, child-rearing, and sexuality. Discussing exo-psychology with a yokel is like discussing sexual experience with a pre-adolescent. S/he just can't understand the new reality because hir neural circuits have not been turned on—and s/he may turn you in for philosophic child-molesting. Pre-mutated humans naturally believe that *Homo sapien's* evolution has already reached its highest stage. The yokel can become passionately moralistic, attacking the post-terrestrial for being elitist, callous to human suffering, antihuman, escapist, even diabolical.

The bland, smiling "hippie" and "yogi body-engineer," the first two transitional stages of post-terrestrial "wingless butterflies," are no longer hooked to social symbols. The Hippie-Zen adept no longer reflexively reacts to the virtue-shame systems by which society domesticates its workers, but has not yet evolved to master newly activated circuits.

CHAPTER 10

SPACE MIGRATION

THE HUMAN SPECIES IS EXPLODING into hundreds of new sub-species. We're learning a great deal about genetic concepts that have to do with migration, the neurology of mutation, swarming, social castes, genepools, neoteny, and terminal adulthood. I consider those who fail to understand the liberating inevitability of space migration with the amused curiosity with which we regard members of the Flat Earth Society or, at best, the gentle Amish who serenely turn their back on technological expansion of intelligence.

Columbus came back to Spain in 1493 and said, "Hey, we can live over there," just as the astronauts came back and said, "Listen, the Moon and high space can be colonized." Now, when the word came back that there was a new continent, a lot of people said, "How dare you go over there? You're copping out. We should stay back here in Europe and build the dome of the Vatican, settle the wars of the Catholics and the Protestants, and fight with the Armada." Others said, "Life as we know it now can't exist over there. It's a primitive, terrible place."

MAL-CONTENTS MIGRATE

MIGRATION TO NORTH AMERICA was self-selective. William Penn and his group of dissenters wanted to get out of England, because they couldn't create Quaker reality there. The Catholic Lord Calvert led a group over because they were being persecuted by the Church of England. The Pilgrim mothers and fathers fled from England to Holland, mortgaged their possessions, and sailed the Mayflower, because they wanted a place to live out the kooky, freaky reality that they collectively shared. And there's no question the experiment is a success. Americans are freer than Europeans, and Westerners are a new species evolving away from Americans. There's more experimentation, more openness, more tolerance of differences, more future orientation in the West.

MUTATIONS DISTURB THE CORE CULTURE.

FREEDOM IS UP

NOW, the ecological Puritans among us say, "Limit growth!" Well, you can't. Who are we to tell every have-not person in Asia, Africa, our country, and South America they can't have two cars in their garages, a color television, skateboards, and snow blowers? Nobody has come up with any plan for full employment, for getting a growth economy without inflation or a war or altering the environment. In the early 1960s Kennedy realized that he couldn't get the country going again unless he moved us up. He said, "We're going to the moon."

One message we've learned from the DNA code is that population growth is out of our control. It's not within our power to really change an evolutionary process two and a half billion years old. We're just robot evolutionary agents, programmed to transport sperm-egg cargoes higher and faster and farther. Population is increasing. Within ten or fifteen or twenty years, some dictator will press a button, and who'd blame him? Space migration is the escape valve.

HOME

WITHIN TEN YEARS after initiating space migration, a group of a thousand people will be able to get together cooperatively and build a new mini-world cheaper than they could buy individual houses down here. Within twenty-five years, there'll be a High Orbital Mini-Earth (HOME) for your vision of social reality. You have the right, duty, and responsibility to externalize that vision with those who share it. The only way you can do that is in a HOME. because there's going to be an increasing poverty of vision down here as we get more populated and as energy decreases.

Space migration is not another cycle of exploration/exploitation. When you've got new ideas you can't hang around the old hive. Space migration is the only way our species can be assured a multiplicity of options in which the next series of experiments in human genetics can occur. Pollution, crowding, and restlessness are the characteristic stimuli for migration. Malcontents migrate.

A lot of people in NASA didn't like me going around talking to people about HOMEs. They were afraid that you'll want it too soon—and get disappointed if they don't deliver fast enough. Still, within NASA there are young space freaks who sincerely want to get this planet moving and provide the increased freedom of space migration.

MIGRANTS SELF-SELECT

THE FABRICATION OF MINI-WORLDS should be voluntary. No government bureau should select who goes into space. Those that want to go, can try. Self-selection, not bureaucratic selection, should be used. Studies of social insects, herd animals, and human migrations all show that some migrate and some stay put. Some restless gene-carriers left the bogsides of Ireland and came to the New World. Most remained, where even to this day they continue their ancient territorial-totem conflicts.

SPACE MIGRATION IS THE ESCAPE VALVE.

Here's a simple ethological experiment anyone can perform. Ask the next hundred people you meet if they would like to inhabit large High Orbital Mini-Earths. Probably at least half of those polled will embrace the idea. About 10% will be immediately enthusiastic. The younger the sample, of course, the higher percentage of aspirations for migration.

Such responses are probably genetic. The idea either does or does not trigger off an "Ah, yes" reaction. The same process has been occurring for centuries. When the migration-to-America idea-signal was flashed in the 16th Century, some nervous systems reflexively flashed "Let's go." Some will be impelled, compelled, obsessed, driven, fired, wired to move into space; others are bone-deeply, cell-essence horrified by the idea. We must listen to and respect these strong reactions.

MIGRATION BENEFITS ALL

THOSE NOT HARD-WIRED TO GO should be assured that migration benefits those who stay put in at least two ways. First, migration is an escape valve that rids

SOME MIGRATE AND SOME STAY PUT. the home hive of restless outcastes. Second, migration allows for new experiments—technological, political, and social—in a new ecological niche far from the home hive. The stay-puts then benefit from the fallout of the frontier mutational experiments. In this context, America can be seen as an enormous selective-breeding genetic experiment performed by Old World gene-pools. When restless-mobile outcastes are allowed to move on, everyone benefits.

WOMEN ACTIVATE

I FIND IT USEFUL TO CONCLUDE DISCUSSIONS about space migration with an appeal to women. The swashbuckling argonaut-astronaut caste always forms the first wave. Once the mysterious frontier is demonstrated to be safe and inhabitable, then the religious and economic bureaucrats move in. But nothing happens until the women are activated. Space migration will explode when women realize that the best place to love, have children, and fabricate new cultures is in a HOME of one's own design.

NOTHING HAPPENS UNTIL WOMEN ACTIVATE.

CHAPTER II

POWER OF SPIN

I ALWAYS SOUGHT TO UNDERSTAND my own behavior and, so far as possible, the actions of others—in terms of particle physicists. The logic seems simple. Everyone agrees that nuclear physicists are the smartest caste of our species. Hence, the cliche "You don't have to be a rocket scentists to...." They had, after all, transmitted matter into energy— $E=mc^2$. As far as I am concerned, the president of the American Physical Society should automatically double as president of the United States.

Nuclear physicists are observing, measuring, and establishing friendly relations with basic units of energy-matter. Quarks seem to be units of information-intelligence. All grosser, slower structures—atoms, molecules, cells, multicelled organisms—are simply frozen bits of nuclear information. It seems logical that the behavior of human beings—including myself—might be explained and understood in terms of the characteristics of quarks.

It was delightful to discover Nobel Prize physicists discussing quarks in terms of charm, magnetic charge, strangeness, and spin—a new concept for psychology. The more I examined the implications of particle-spin for human meaning, the clearer it became that "spin" is a psychological idea whose time had come.

Politicians readily use spin doctors. Nuclear reactors and space technology have made us experientially aware that everything in nature, from galaxies to mesons to the drainage from your sink, is merrily revolving both around its own personal axis and in orbital paths around everything else—everything spins

For centuries, we human beings have known that our planet rotates around its axis every 24 hours and around the sun one revolution per year. But not until recent satellite pictures could we "feel" the little sphere busily rotating from west to east—an amazing amount of survival data and evolutionary significance associated with East versus West orientation.

In terms of spherical geometry, the 30th to 45th degrees latitude—North and South—locate the runways along which gene-pools accelerate to escape velocity. North-South is an astro-neurological constant based on magnetic charge. East-West is an astro-neurological constant based on spin. Rotational orientation relative to the home star determines the direction of migrating intelligence.

FEEL THE SPIN

To EXPERIENCE THE POWER OF SPIN, imagine that you stand 50 miles—250,000 feet—high above sea level. Face west and sense the Earth moving you backwards. You would have to keep striding forward

1,000 miles an hour to keep the sun at the same angle—an easy stroll at 100 paces an hour would do it. Face east and feel that you are moving downward, pushed by spin-momentum, at 1,000 miles an hour. You are falling towards the sun, which will rise in front of you, below you.

Primitive organisms face the sun. They ride passively towards the sun. More advanced organisms develop the mobility to chase the sun, to move against the rotational tide. When you greet the sun, after the night, you are facing Asia. The word "Asia," which comes from Greek-Latin, means "region of the rising sun," whereas the word "Europe" comes from Greek and Semitic, means "land of the setting sun." When you face east, you are peering down into the past where our gene-pools came from. When you see the sun disappear over the horizon, you are looking up into the future. This basic attitudinal orientation based on spin is one of the fundamental define—characteristics of all energy structures.

AS ABOVE, SO BELOW

THE HERMETIC DOCTRINE HOLDS that what is so above, is so below. Recapitulation theory holds that the same sequences re-evolve at all levels of energy. Neurologic thus leads us to expect spin to be a basic dimension of biological structure. To understand a terrestrial human, it is necessary to understand hir spin-caste, determined by how far west s/he and hir gene-pool have migrated—and at what speed.

92 PERCENT OF OTHER PEOPLE ARE
AT DEVELOPMENTAL A STAGE
DIFFERENT FROM YOURS.

FORE-SPIN; BACK-SPIN

FORE-SPIN IS MOVING WEST, pushing up against the rotation to develop mobility, to attain altitude—moving into the future, ascending into empty ecological niches. Why was California explored and settled from Europe? Why didn't the wisdom of the East sail across the Pacific? Why today do the eastern countries compress into xenophobic, centralized anthills, discouraging migration?

The answer is simple. It is because of back-spin—sitting, immobile, passively riding the down-wave. Occidental-orientation is actively pushing against rotation, continually being tested, shaped, and formed by the airflow. Your antennae is continually probing forward for the next pathway opening up.

BEHAVIOR OF HUMAN BEINGS CAN BE UNDERSTOOD IN TERMS OF THE CHARACTERISTICS OF QUARKS.

Only from post-terrestrial altitude can one realize that on a spinning sphere, going against the spin is "up." Try this: Turn a world map so that East is down. Then imagine the long climb of humanity from East to West. The busy caravans shuttling up and down the Asian trade routes. Picture the enormous ant-armies of Alexander overrunning the past, leaving him with no worlds for him to conquer westward. Think of Genghis Khan's fast-moving equine technology storming upward. See the explosion of Muslim columns and Roman legions painfully pushing up into Gaul. Sense the movement of human swarms over the centuries—the empire-hives sending out the exploratory probes westward. For 1,000 years—A.D. 400 to 1400—the waves of mobile-elite sperm-eggs splashed up to the western-European beachledges and waited to scale the Atlantic Ocean—the greatest swarming phenomenon in human history! The port-cities of Cadiz, Lisbon, and London teemed with migrants, explorers, and space-travelers commanded by a genetic directive to scale this mountain of water 3,000 miles high.

During the 10 centuries before Columbus, doughty Vikings and fervent Irish monks returned to tell the story of the new ecological niche. But the technology for lifting gene-pools into the unknown had not emerged. The Atlantic Ascent had to await the Protestant Reformation to free gene-pools from the Catholic-hive center. Only a society of self-actualized families, democratically linked together, was capable of pushing gene-pools into the storm altitudes of the North Atlantic.

GENETIC INTELLIGENCE

A GENE-POOL IS A SPECIES-UNIT capable of protecting its young over several generations. Marauding Francis Drakes, John Waynes, and John Glenns are beginning probes, but nothing happens until the family units move together.

Genetic intelligence is measured by the ability to move gene-pools upward, angling always westward, pushing against, and being shaped, re-formed, activated, mutated by spin-pressure from the future.

THE FOOL ON THE HILL WATCHES THE SUN
GO DOWN AND THE EYES IN HIS HEAD
WATCH THE WORLD GO 'ROUND.
- THE BEATLES

CHAPTER 12

TERRESTRIAL

POLITICS

TERRESTRIAL POLITICS is based on mammalian competitions between neighboring hives that share the same neurotechnological level. Each quantum jump in neurotechnology increases the size of the political unit. Tribes are swallowed up by neighbors with superior artifacts. Higher-technology nations set up boundaries of greater extension. China and Russia confronted each other along a 3,000-mile border with the same nervous, bluffing postures of four-footed mammals protecting turf.

Ideological differences are, of course, irrelevant. Neighboring gene-pools have to compete according to a relentless law of territorial—plus-minus—magnetism. To occupy any ecological niche is automatically to be "against" those who inhabit the neighboring one.

TO UNDERSTAND A TERRESTRIAL HUMAN STUDY HIR SPIN-CASTE.

Middle East alliances in the latter 20th Century illustrate the limbic, primitive-brain, nature of Old World politics. Morocco received its arms from America; its neighbor, Algeria, obtained weapons from enemies of America. The border between the two neighbors was always tense. The next country, Tunisia, received arms from America and quarrels with both its leftist neighbors, Algeria and Libya. Poor, confused Egypt switched from Russia to America and managed to maintain hostile contact with both its neighbors—Libya and Israel, regardless of ideology.

Continuing down the zoo-cages of our animal past, note that with an amazing disregard for common sense or political principles, each country opposes its neighbors.

Such a renowned political theorist as Henry Kissinger was so totally robotized that he believed in the Domino Theory: If South Vietnam fell, then all the Southeast Asian nations would topple into monolithic communism. The paranoia completely disregarded the obvious. Once Saigon collapsed, nature took over! Cambodia attacked Vietnam, Vietnam raided Laos, Thailand snarled at Vietnam—and all Southeast Asian countries opposed their northern neighbor, China. Africa revealed the same confrontations. The political map of Africa concealed the fact that within countries arbitrarily defined by European colonists, tribal enmities rage on. Africa is a checkerboard of mammalian savagery. Ninety percent of African countries are ruled by assassins and military chiefs.

TO OCCUPY ANY ECOLOGICAL NICHE IS AUTOMATICALLY TO BE "AGAINST" THOSE WHO INHABIT THE NEIGHBORING ONE.

SAME PATTERN

UNTIL WORLD WAR II, Europe was also a checker-board of quarreling neighbors. The technological quantum-leap, which always increases the size of the gene-pool territory, forced a change. The Eastern Bloc nations were forced together into a monolith confronting the union of West European states. Border tensions no longer exist between nations except along the great East-West Iron Curtain. Note, also, that 90% of West European countries are ruled by elected representatives.

This North-South bifurcation of the genetic highway has produced a fascinating left-right division that perfectly parallels the cerebral hemispheric split. The "right-hand" northern countries developed logic, rationality, manipulation of artifacts and symbols. New technologies require harmonious collaboration. The energies of thousands must be linked up to maintain an automotive business or a Coca-Cola industry. Technology creates larger and more intelligent gene-colony units.

Why did the right-hand Europe develop the technology and carry the freedom-gene upward? Why did the left-hand Africa fail to produce mobility-freedom-gene-pools? Why did the genetic highway veer north instead of south when it burst out of the Middle East? Why did the northern Mediterranean centers—Greece, Rome, Venice, Paris, Madrid, Lisbon, London—light up in sequence?

EVOLUTIONARY ASCENT

THINK OF EVOLUTION AS AN ASCENT—literally a climb, a series of intelligence tests that activate the velocity-altitude-freedom circuits. From the Mid-East midbrain there are two pathways. The Arabs took the easiest, the southern route and slid off along the low road. Insectoid armies oozing from the east, sending soldiers and military bureaucrats.

The high-road North was a ladder to be scaled. Look at the map: First the Dardanelles to be crossed, then the prickly mountains of Greece, the fingered peninsulas, the Balkan mountains, the high Alps' rugged land, choked with geographic barriers offering refuge to ascending gene-pools. The story of evolution is the ascent of Celtic out-castes on the shoulders of the teeming Eastern autonomic-involuntary centers.

A glance at the map reminds us that the human race is exactly a competition of speed: Small gene-pools racing to keep ahead of the engulfing wave of insectoid collectivism. Swarming pressures squirt small gene-pools into empty ecological niches where new realities, "Plan-Its," can be created.

The issue is never in doubt, however. The primitive past lapping at the outskirts of the frontier is simply a signal to speed up. When Socialist-equality becomes dogma, genetic-elitism reappears among the Western out-castes, and new gene-pools assemble on the frontier outposts. Everyone on the frontier is self-selected for frontier behavior. The new ecological niche is always filled by those genetically templated for mobility, independence, and change. The ascent of gene-pools up the Atlantic was a gigantic genetic-selection process. Typically, each European gene-pool sent its best fertile stock. Once a beachhead had been established, more settled members of the gene-pools could follow. But in most cases, new gene-pools were formed by mutated migrants.

CHAPTER 13

CASTE

DiViSioN

CASTE DIVISION is a most effective survival device. A species with caste differentiation and enculturation based on multistage imprinting—obvious examples: social insects and humans—divides its survival specialties, thus complexifying and expanding performance.

STRUCTURAL CASTES

ETHOLOGISTS DESCRIBE two forms of caste differentiation: structural and temporal. Structural caste is defined by genetic wiring: division into specialized functions—worker, warrior, drone, builder—that characterized hive organisms and civilized hum-ants. Structural caste in insects is easily identified by visible morphological or anatomical differences. A drone bee looks different from a worker or queen. Highly complex neurological differences also characterize each insect hive. The nervous system of each juvenile worker-ant is imprinted with specific culture cues.

CASTE DIVISION IS A MOST EFFECTIVE SURVIVAL DEVICE.

In humans, however, neurological differences are more important in determining the behavior of each caste. Genetic-anatomical templating produces involuntary-robot behaviors. Male and female is one structural caste difference. Big, muscled, hyperadrenalized aggressives are a separate caste—the warriors, the Amazons. Dainty, fragile, nurturant minister-types are a caste.

Bobby Fischers, J. Edgar Hoovers, Bella Abzugs, and Marilyn Monroes are caste-exemplars. The caste distinctions are blatantly visible.

CASTE DISTINCTIONS ARE BLATANTLY VISIBLE.

Although these differences were taken for granted by earlier societies, discussion of genetic types is taboo among modern humans—it's "politically incorrect." Socialist countries forbid talk about genetic caste-differences because Marxism holds that society determines behavior. Western democracies deny caste differences because of commitment to equality. Revulsion against Nazi fanaticism also makes genetic caste discussions verboten among liberals—and most scientists are liberals. It is interesting that uneducated, lower-class people readily accept the reality of racial and caste differences. Country bumpkins and illiterate farmers are aware of the obvious effects of breeding. Common sense suggests that new caste differences will emerge as *Homo sapiens* continue their accelerated evolution.

TEMPORAL CASTES

TEMPORAL CASTE REFERS TO THE PROCESS of maturation in which an individual metamorphoses from one form to another, performing different survival functions at each developmental stage.

In an anthill, temporal casting assigns the young tasks of infant care. Slightly older ants are assigned housekeeping and hive-repair functions, metamorphosing into the more external functions of exploration, food-gathering, or warrior activity. An organism that has passed through temporal metamorphic sequences is simply more intelligent. Temporal caste means polyphase brain and, thus, multiple realities. The suckling infant is certainly a very different caste from the serious 10-year-old school child. The rock' n' roll teenager is certainly a different caste from the tottering post-menopausal.

Until recently, our philosophers have been unable to understand temporal casting in humans—for very good genetic reasons. At each developmental stage, the individual must imprint the current hive-reality for that stage. The infant is not concerned with teenage preoccupations. Each human accepts the reality of the current temporal stage hive-imprint and almost totally represses the memory of previous stages. Senior citizens forget what it was like to be adolescents.

Think of the human gene-pool as a complex molecule that builds on new elements as it evolves. Temporal casting allows for temporal flexibility. Each generation is a wave moving through the gene-pool—contributing to the locomotion of the gene-pool through time. Does the suckling infant play a role in the human anthill? Oh, yes! The infant's task is to trigger domestic responses in adults. The neonate performing its repertoire of activities is working just as hard as the auto worker or the dutiful parent.

PEOPLE ON THE FRONTIER ARE SELF-
SELECTED FOR FRONTIER BEHAVIOR.

SIGNIFICANCE OF THE PILL

IF MOM'S BRAIN WERE NOT CUED by gurgles and cries, she would be down at the dance hall swinging her hips—or horrors!—competing with men. Thus the enormous neurogenetic significance of the Pill. An irresistible Women's Liberation Movement occurs one generation after voluntary

NEW TECHNOLOGIES REQUIRE HARMONIOUS COLLABORATION.

birth control appears. Birth control is self-directed management of temporal caste sequence. Women can postpone matron-morality. The "youth-cult" which has produced middle-aged teeny boppers and married teamsters wearing Fonz hair styles is another by-product of the newly-won control of our neurogenetic brain sequences.

The school child—ages 5-11—plays a crucial role in keeping the educational industry going. The teenager caste plays a warrior role. Indeed, every dictator knows how to keep restless students from rioting in the university—get them fighting on the border. In times of peace, urbanoid teenagers keep the police and the judiciary going. More than half of all reported crimes are committed by those under 18. Every caste has to be kept occupied. In "primitive" tribes, young children perform baby care. Older girls help with agriculture, older boys guard the flocks. Civilized society's technology and complex labor divisions have diminished the survival value of child-castes leading to the elaborate extended education to prepare youngsters for warrior and post-warrior status.

CHAPTER 14
PRiMiTiVE
REALiTY STAGES

THE CRUCIAL SCIENTIFIC QUESTION is this: What are the stages of human evolution—both in the species and in the individual? Most human conflict and confusion could be sweetly solved if we understood that 92 percent of other human beings—and societies—are at developmental stages different from our own. To know all is to forgive all. We smile tolerantly at younger kids because we know we passed through those stages and that they will too.

Knowledge of human stages allows us to smile at the hunter-gatherers in our society who expect welfare checks and are great at running and jumping; to tolerate the passionate, dramatic rhetoric of Mideastern midbrainers; to comfort domesticated parents worrying about their kids; to support advanced brain computer-electronic wizards who have activated brain circuits ahead of ours. The answer to all human problems is to recognize your genetic stage, go to the place where your genetic peers hang out, and in that secure place prepare yourself for the future stages inevitably awaiting you.

We need a scientific and psychologically convincing list of human states. This search must take into account the fact that for the last 5,000 years, the shrewdest ethologists and philosophers have been typecasting human behavior on the basis of extensive empirical evidence. These ancient classifications, which must have some validity, have produced the classic typologies of human castes–the 12 signs of the Zodiac, the 22 Tarot types, the 12 Graeco-Roman divinities– which clearly represent basic human modalities.

THE ZODIAC PRESENTS 12 SURVIVAL TACTICS.

THE ZODIAC

THE ZODIAC PRESENTS 12 SURVIVAL TACTICS, each of which refers to a genetic technology and a development stage. Suppose we study the correspondences between the original sequence of the Zodiac and the stage of evolution which science defines for our species and us as individuals.

In the incoherent tangle of Zodiac ravings, we find three important items of neurogenetic wisdom. First, regular cycles influence neural development. Second, each of us is controlled by rhythms we can decipher. Third, we harmonize with the cycles.

Each of us is born into a caste, or a complex of castes, that we pass through as we mature. To attempt correspondence between astrology and science is doubly risky. Scientists scornfully consider astrology as superstition. Astrologers prudishly resent scientists intruding on their symbols. But no matter.

EVOLVING THROUGH THE SIGNS

LET US ASSUME FOR A MOMENT that each of us represents one of the twelve intelligence-survival-solutions and that each of us, in maturing, passes through and relives all twelve solutions. This clever tactic allows each of us to recapitulate evolution and to move ahead to create the future. Individual human beings evolve, stage by stage, as higher circuits of the CNS are activated. Our 24-calibre brain allows us to imprint or fabricate temporal "Realities" available to every major life-form that has preceded us on the scene. We can creatively reimprint each of the 24 temporal realities.

THE TWELVE REALTIES

STAGE 1: WELCOME TO THE PLANET. Your first assignment is to suck, float, turn your amoeboid receptors towards the warm breast and incorporate chemicals that will make you grow.

STAGE I RECEPTIVE-DEPENDENT INFANT	Zodiac—Pieces
	Species—Amoebid
	Bio-stage—Sucking
	Tarot—Fool
	Trigram—*Kun*-Earth
	Divinity—Pluto-Proserpine
	Eco-niche—Water

STAGE 2: AT ABOUT SIX MONTHS OLD you can define yourself a self-mobile, incisive, shark-like individual pushing towards and away from what you want to put in your baby mouth.

STAGE 2 BITING- SQUIRMING INFANT	Zodiac—Aries
	Species—Fish
	Bio-stage—Biting
	Tarot—Magus
	Trigram—*Kun*-Earth
	Divinity—Neptune
	Eco-niche—Water

STAGE 3: HEY, YOU MADE IT to the shore-line-floor-line. At about one year old you are ready to cut loose from Sea-Mother and slowly, steadily start to master gravity.

STAGE 3 CRAWLING INFANT	Zodiac—Taurus
	Species—Amphibian
	Bio-stage—Crawling
	Tarot—Empress
	Trigram—*Kun*-Earth
	Divinity—Ceres-Dionysus
	Eco-niche—Shoreline

STAGE 4: CONGRATULATIONS! Moving into this stage between one and two years old you can precariously stand up on your two legs and use your bipedal neurotechnology to scurry around like a clever, tricky rodent grabbing everything you can get your hands on when they're not looking.

MANY SCIENTIFIC CONCEPTS WERE ANTICIPATED BY THE OCCULT SYSTEM OF THE PAST.

STAGE 4 TODDLER	Zodiac—Gemini
	Species—Rodent
	Bio-stage—Toddler
	Tarot—High Priestess
	Trigram—Ch'en-Earthquake
	Divinity—Hermes-Mercury
	Eco-niche—Low-land

STAGE 5: OH, HO! At two to three years old, you're big and crafty enough to stake out and defend your little claim. Your crib, your doll, your room, your Mommy. Nervous, jumpy, possessive mammal. Feeling your size, especially with the littler ones. Just three years old and you're a mafla-capo, a treacherous lion, a power-jumpy politician. More power to you, kid. Thanks for the smile.

STAGE 5 TERRITORIAL CHILD	Zodiac—Cancer
	Species—Carnivore
	Bio-stage—Territorial Kid
	Tarot—Emperor
	Trigram—Ch'en-Earthquake
	Divinity—Vesta
	Eco-niche—High-land

STAGE 6: BIG DEAL, BIG SHOT. By three to four years old you've learned that gesture, grimace, cry, posture, exhibitionist noise can attract attention, signal your needs. You're talking, but it's monkey noises and birdcalls. But it works, and you're pretty pleased with your power to communicate.

STAGE 6 SHOW OFF ID	Zodiac—Leo
	Species—Primate
	Bio-stage—Gesturing Kid
	Tarot—High Priest
	Trigram—*Kan*-Toil
	Divinity—Apollo
	Eco-niche—Trees

STAGE 7: AT ABOUT AGE FOUR TO SIX YEARS OLD the fun begins: you learn word-magic. You catch on that you can speak or write certain words and, boy, something happens! You are now a six-year-old with the mind of a paleolith savage. You don't understand how or why, but the ritual action works.

Most of the 21st Century humanity remains at this pre-semantic level. At least fifty percent of Americans don't think for themselves; indeed they have been educated by society not to think for themselves, but to rote-learn and parrot.

STAGE 7 PARROTING MIMICKER	Zodiac—Virgo
	Species—Paleolith
	Bio-stage—Parroting Kid
	Tarot—Lovers
	Trigram—*Kan*-Toil
	Divinity—Diana
	Eco-niche—Caves

STAGE 8: BY SIX TO EIGHT YEARS OLD you've learned how to use words as tools, rearrange them logically, invent new combinations, figure things out on your own, and think for yourself! As a seven-year old, you have attained the mentality of a neolithic toolmaker.

STAGE 8 THINKING KID	Zodiac—Libra
	Species—Neolith Metal-age
	Bio-stage—Thinking Kid
	Tarot—Chariot
	Trigram—*Kan*-Toil
	Divinity—Prometheus
	Eco-niche—Huts

STAGE 9: AT NINE TO TWELVES YEARS OLD you are learning how to play collaboratively, join groups, divide labor, take part in organized teams. You have reached the tribal level of species evolution. You are still a superstitious, treacherous savage, but you are on the way to becoming a civilized human-insectoid.

STAGE 9 GROUP ACTIVITY	Zodiac—Scorpio
	Species—Tribal
	Bio-stage—Gang Kid
	Tarot—Strength
	Trigram—*Kan*-Toil
	Divinity—Minerva
	Eco-niche—Village

STAGE 10: DURING THE TEENAGED YEARS you're really cooking. The sexual-courtship-mating circuits of your brain have been activated by RNA hormones. You're a teenage robot, obsessed with your identity. You're romantic, intense, cruel, moody, emotional, fickle, not yet socialized, wary, rebellious of those who wish to civilize you. And you love to laugh at adults.

STAGE 10 ADOLESCENT BARBARERISM	
	Zodiac—Sagittarius
	Species—Feudal
	Bio-stage—Gang Kid
	Tarot—Strength
	Trigram—*Kan*-Toil
	Divinity—Mars-Venus
	Eco-niche—City

STAGE 11: UH, OH. WHAT HAPPENED? You've been tamed—without realizing it. All at once, you of all people have become an adult. You've got a job, settled down, given up your wild, romantic dreams. The territorial circuits in your brain have been activated. You're a domesticated robot. You want to get a piece of turf, lock into a hive-task, be part of society and settle down. Build a little nest. Get married. The parenting instinct is going to lock you up. You are an adult.

STAGE 11 DOMESTICATED ADULT	Zodiac—Capricorn Species—Democracy Bio-stage—Adult-Parent Tarot—Wheel Trigram—Ken-Protection Divinity—Juno-Jupiter Eco-niche—Industrial

STAGE 12: WOW, WHERE DID YOUR LIFE GO? It all spun by so fast. For twenty years you've been a parent-slave, obsessed with child-care, working, struggling to protect the young. Now they've grown and gone and the old energy juices aren't flowing. You've lost fire and vigor. You are no longer interested in change, competition. You sense aging, weakness approaching. You feel vulnerable and scared. You try to cling to the past, but it's all changing and you're not sure you like it. You can't protect yourself anymore. You look for security. You want a strong government, Social Security, and police-establishment to take care of you. You think you're gonna die.

STAGE 12 SENIOR CITIZEN	Zodiac—Aquarius Species—Centralized State Bio-stage—Elder Tarot—Justice Trigram—Ken-Protection Divinity—Themis Eco-niche—Humanoid Hive

CHAPTER 15
FUTURE STAGES
OF EVOLUTION

S O FAR, THIS LIST OF TEMPORAL STAGES of human life is fairly standard. But now we shall consider, possibly for the first time, a systematic prediction of twelve stages of human evolution to come! There have been sporadic previous attempts to forecast human development, such as the Purgatorid and Paradisio of Dante, for example. Various utopian and science fiction writers have described their futique visions, such as in Robert Heinlein's *Future History* series.

The next paragraphs present the first logical, empirical sequence of future steps, based on scientific facts and corresponding to sequences of ordinality presented in many philosophic systems of the past, including the *I Ching*, the Tarot-numeration, the Zodiac, Greco-Roman divinities, Hebrew alphabet, as well as the ordination presented in the *Periodic Table of Elements*, the unfolding chronology of scientific and technological discoveries in neurology, biochemistry, microgenetics, and quantum physics.

Recall that at the onset of our researches in consciousness-expanding drugs we revised the Buddhist-Tibetan *Book of the Dead* and the *Tao Te Ching* and even the Catholic ritual of the mass to fit into modern brain-change. The experts in these fields tended to dismiss our bridging gestures as "sacrilege."

If scientists believe in the orderly evolution of knowledge, they, too, should be please to discover that the most up-to-date concepts of wholistic body consciousnessness, neuroelectronics, genetics-sociobiology, and quantum physics where anticipated, however metaphorically, by the occult system of the past.

PROGNOSTICATION

THE FOLLOWING LIST OF PROGNOSTICATION is immediately and practically applicable to your life. It sets up a specific sequence of self-growth. This is, therefore, the first program of individual development to specify how the intelligent human can follow a schedule of inner development correlating with the astonishing and liberating advances in external science.

When we have mastered those first twelve primitive, survival techniques and can handle the unfolding 21st Century social realities, we are ready to pass through the steps of post-cultural, post-bureaucratic, self-confident, self-contained, and self-direction.

STAGE 13: YOUR ABILITY TO AVOID, compassionately and humorously, the limits of your social-hive, allows you to define yourself as an aesthetic consumer. Your body belongs to you. You must learn to relax, transcend the guilty-pessimism of prescientific religions, become a sensually receptive, artistically indolent, passively-hip pleasure-lover. Rejoice in your ability to live as an esthetic dilettante, a neurological gourmet, a happy-go-lucky hippie, wandering through the Judeo-Christian garden of eden.

STAGE 13	Zodiac—Pisces
HEDONIC	Species—Hedonic Consumer
CONSUMER	Bio-stage—Me-generation
	Tarot—Hang Man
	Trigram—*Tui*-Joyous Lake
	Divinity—Tethys
	Eco-niche—Receptive Body

Now you must resist 2,000 years of grim pressure to make you into a slave of society. Hedonic consumerism is a stage you are going through. Like sucking infancy, like careless adolescence, you are not going to remain at this level forever. But you must master the sensual, erotic instruments of your body, use your sensorium as a complex mosaic of rapture, understand how to indulge and pleasure yourself.

STAGE 14: WHEN YOU ARE CLEVER ENOUGH, and diligent enough to get your sensory-somatic scene together, you can advance to this simple and playful next step. You have taken the great, basic step by freeing yourself from the hive-morality of submission-suffering. Now you start creating an esthetic environment around you. You will have lots of help. There are thousands of texts, manuals, courses, teachers to assist you, to offer leads and methods.

The only danger is that you might get caught in one style. In your liberated exuberance, you may sign up too quickly in one mode of self-actualization. Scout out the field. For thousands of years the most intelligent, free, strong people have been fabricating personal esthetic realities. Don't fall for the first neighborhood master. Remember, to keep developing in the future, there is only one trap to avoid: loss of faith in yourself, your own tough, innocent potential to grow.

STAGE 14	Zodiac—Aries
HEDONIC	Species—Hedonic Engineer
ARTIST	Bio-stage—Body Intelligence
	Tarot—Death
	Trigram—*Tui*-Joyous Lake
	Divinity—Oceanus
	Eco-niche—Self-Managed Body

During this stage you learn to make your life a work of art, a quiet, smiling dance of growing beauty. There is no hurry. Each esthetic yoga takes time—the complexity of your somatic and neural equipment is infinite and unique. Also, as you continue to evolve, you will constantly add to your esthetic style. Indeed, each stage beyond simple Esthetic Mastery requires that you go back and improve, simplify, complicate your growing singularity.

STAGE 15: AFTER YOU HAVE LOCATED THE SOURCE OF VIRTUE and pleasure within yourself and learned how to create external projections of your inner style, you are ready to take the next logical step in personal development. Link up with another or others.

At this point we can look back and see that the Consciousness movements of the 1960s brought millions of Americans and Western Europeans through the stages of hedonic consumer and hedonic artist. If you remain at hedonic consumer, you're a lazy hippie. If you remain in lonely splendor at Hedonic Artist, a narcissist. Both are steps to pass through.

STAGE 15	Zodiac—Taurus
ESTHETIC	Species—Tantric Union
LINKAGE	Bio-stage—Hedonic Link-up
	Tarot—Temperance
	Trigram—*Tui*-Joyous Lake
	Divinity—Rhea
	Eco-niche—Body Fusion

The inclination to club, to fuse, to link-up with others who share your esthetic style is the obvious progression. Symbiosis, grouping is the way that isolated DNA organisms formed the first cells. Social grouping led us from the caves to a new order-linkage based not just on economics or territorial defense, but for shared esthetic vision—a new social connection of free, confident individuals whose aim is to enhance personal growth, to stimulate in each other inner development, to turn each other on, to add to each other's hedonic progress.

The ancient name for this stage is tantra, fusion of the erotic-spiritual-psychological. Usually this occurs au pair—two enlightened people discover that one-times-one equals infinity. Often larger groups assemble for esthetic-lifestyle sharing: communes, intentional communities, esthetic groups who work-play together around a common artistic task.

ADVANCED STAGES

STAGE 16: THE STAGES TO COME make great demands upon one's strength and confidence. It is almost impossible to maintain a solitary life of continual mutation-metamorphosis. The support and balance and broadened perspective of the shared-voyage require conscious fusion. These linkages need not be possessive. Often two or more people join, exchange the energy-insight needed to master the stage and then, lovingly, part to explore varied new realms of the future.

STAGE 16 NEUROLOGICAL ELECTRONIC CONSUMER	
Zodiac—Gemini	
Species—Neuro-electronic Consumer	
Bio-stage—Self-Indulgence	
Tarot—Devil	
Trigram—Li-Fire	
Divinity—Theia	
Eco-niche—Brain-computer Link	

At rare and wonderful times in human history, societies have emerged affluent and secure enough to allow certain intelligent individuals the freedom to explore the three stages just described. The history of art and civilization is the story of what can be done with the body, its sense-organs, and musculature. Lucky you! You're living in the greatest electric-brain boom of all time.

Since World War II an entirely new dimension of human neurotechnology has developed. Radio, television, high-fidelity reception, high-speed calculators and computers have activated dramatically and advanced your brain-response-accelerated and expanded the scope of your reception, integration, and transmission of signals. The suburban child of five has experienced a million times more realities than the most educated-traveled aristocrat before 1940. The revolutionary advances in transportation, including extraterrestrial rocketry, have also stretched human neurology.

BRAIN ACCELERATION

THE SUDDEN EXPLOSION of brain-activating drugs in the 1960s was a natural consequence of this neuroelectronic information processing. While around four percent of those growing up in our electronic computer culture are genetically equipped with brains that can instinctively harmonize with accelerated computer rhythms, the rest of us require chemical assistance, a brain-activating drug which will free our brains to move at the speed and breadth of the information presented by electronic devices. We need neuro-acceleration aids to keep up with the computer whiz kids.

During the sixties, millions of people ingested brain-accelerating drugs and exposed themselves to mind-blowing audiovisual overloads. This wow produced a now-generation of passive neuroelectronic consumers who grooved on the McLuhan multiplicity, Futuristic Space Odysseys, who saw protean realities flash on their cerebral projectors, but could not make it work in our own lives. Thus the great retreat back to hot-tub, wholistic hedonism.

But we didn't quit, did we? We were just taking a Me-generation breather. We haven't come this far to spend the rest of our lives as spectators of the cosmo-genetic moving-picture show. So we mutate.

STAGE 17: HEY, HURRAY! At this stage we realize that the universe is not a heavy, gravitational mosaic of stellar-stones or solar-fusion-furnaces, but a web of radiant information. $E=mc^2$; and energy is not Newtonian force-work, but bits of fast-moving decipherable intelligence. Reality is moving pictures filtered through a wide-lens brain, and God (i.e., you) directs the action, writes the script, selects the locations, casts the players, arranges the distribution and promotion.

STAGE 17	Zodiac—Cancer
NEURO-	Species—Neuro-electronic Intelligence
ELECTRONIC	Bio-stage—Brain Wizard
ARTIST	Tarot—Tower
	Trigram—Li-Fire
	Divinity—Cronus
	Eco-niche—Open Post-hive Brain

The successful consumer of external electronics—TV and personal computers—and internal signaling—entheogens—is no longer satisfied to be a passive recipient To evolve in harmony with the times, we must learn how to master the fast-moving equipment-neuro-computers actively assessing the libraries of the world, transmitting via home video, playing complex computer games, using bio-feedback circuitry, accelerating our brains to faster rhythms.

We must all become news anchors. These days there are swarms of Tesla-type "idiot savants" and 17th Stage, 21st Century brains popping up, producing amazing advanced, futique neurological tools. Let's use them.

STAGE 18: AND ONCE we manage high-speed information transmitters, we can free ourselves from our landlocked, terrestrial status. Now that intelligence—not fire-power, humanpower, land-power—is the key to survival, we are ready to leave the surface of the planet and move into high-orbit. Our species could not have reached the moon if we did not have mastery of long-distance, high-speed communication. The landlocked social groupings to defend turf or to control natural resources are no longer relevant once we have access to unlimited space and the natural resources of the moon and asteroid belt.

STAGE 18 NEURO-ELECTRONIC LINKAGE	
	Zodiac—Leo
	Species—Brain-to-Brain Fusion
	Bio-stage—Synergic Mind-link
	Tarot—Star
	Trigram—Li-Fire
	Divinity—Hyperion
	Eco-niche—Space Colonies

Intelligence is high-speed communication and transportation which allows us to form more efficient linkages with others of our kind. This is a definition of love. High fidelity fusion. Aren't we wonderful!

STAGE 19: EVER SINCE the first neolithic agricultural settlements, we have understood the importance of breeding to produce desired life forms. It was the herdsman tribes which developed the first moralities and social structures based on kinship, protection by males, and the egg-supply of the tribe.

For millennia humans have manipulated sperm-egg exchanges to protect and control—a kind of sperm intelligence. Not only our sexual mores but even our theories of evolution have been based on grabbing egg-supplies. The Darwinian theories of evolution suggest that male competition for breeding dominance is the mechanism of evolution. Natural selection is a concept of genetic consumerism; take what is there.

STAGE 19 **GENETIC** **CONSUMERISM**	Zodiac—Virgo **Species**—Genetic Consumer **Bio-stage**—Sperm Intelligence **Tarot**—Moon **Trigram**—*Sun*-Wind **Divinity**—Phoebe **Eco-niche**—RNA-DNA

Deciphering of the DNA code—which occurred exactly at the time when physics decoded the atom, pharmacologists decoded and synthesized brain chemicals, and electronic information-processing emerged on the scene—initiated the era of Genetic Consciousness. The Biological Revolution! Like jubilant adolescent schoolboys, our scientists started recombining DNA strands, cloning, histocompatibility typing, developing DNA repair techniques. Whoops. By reshuffling the chromosomes we can select the new species that we desire. Most exciting is the probability, indeed, the inevitability, that we can decipher the aging sequences and inoculate ourselves against aging and death.

Consumer access to DNA is the ultimate dream of primitive human life. We have attained the status of the Old Testament God—the Father, the immortal creator and controller of life. Welcome to the club.

STAGE 20: BUT WAIT A MOMENT—next is egg wisdom. In our enthusiasm to breed our animals, manage our family gene-pool, manipulate the codes of life, we have made that same classic consumer error, which we committed when we accepted word magic, feudal power, body rapture, and electronic passivity.

STAGE 20 GENETIC INTELLIGENCE	
	Zodiac—Libra
	Species—Genetic Intelligence
	Bio-stage—Egg Wisdom
	Tarot—Sun
	Trigram—*Sun*-Wind
	Divinity—Mnemosyne
	Eco-niche—Genetic Engineering

Sperm intelligence is a stage through which we must joyfully pass. The next step in our development is to realize that there is a biological wisdom that fabricated DNA, that designed us so that we could become smart enough to decipher the code.

Here we return to the pre-urban, pagan wisdom that recognized that there is a genetic intelligence that provided us with the DNA toys with which we play. Scientific paganism is a worshipful respect for biological intelligence and the Gala principle which we are now coming to specify and understand.

We discover that this green, lush planet, protected all comfy and cozy like a cotton womb, with exactly the right temperature and atmosphere and the flow of chemicals arriving exactly where they are needed for DNA to build bodies, is not an inexplicable accident. A wonderful intelligence has been at work to terraform a rocky lunar-like sphere into a Garden of Life.

Gala scientists, like Lovelock and Margulis, have demonstrated that there is one DNA tree of life which operates basically at the unicellular level and which constructs larger organisms as transportation organs to move cells and chemicals around.
Whoops, what's happened? We suddenly realize that we humans are not Father Gods, but humble and grateful agents of the great life web. We are in the wonderful position of being the nervous system of the biological energy. S/He sees what s/he is doing across the galaxy and around the planet through hir continual expansion and to share hir delight in the endless variety of hir beautiful forms.

Now isn't that the best job we've ever been offered? Conscious evolutionary agent! Isn't that the best role we have been cast for in any of the philosophic scenarios? And it's all based on up-to-date evolutionary science.

STAGE 21: AFTER WE GOT CONTROL OF OUR BODIES, we linked-up and got access to our brains. With DNA linkage we got control of our brains, we linked-up and got access to DNA. Now that we understand our genetic function, we can and must link up to continue the process of our own evolution. Symbio-sis is the secret of life. Each single cell is the clubbing of at least three separate DNA species who form cooperative arrangements to construct and maintain that incredible urban complexity—the single cell. The logical momentum of our journey so far and our scientific knowledge of how DNA operates leads us to the conviction that symbiosis, at the DNA level, is an inevitable step in our growth.

I feel good and clear about the first 20 stages of evolution because I have experienced them and science has confirmed my intuitions. But DNA symbiosis is a stage which I have not reached yet and which our geneticists have not worked out yet.

STAGE 21	Zodiac—Scorpio
GENETIC	**Bio-Structure**—Genetic Symbiosis
SYMBIOSIS	**Bio-stage**—DNA Linkage
	Tarot—Judgement
	Trigram—*Chien*-Creative-Heaven
	Divinity—Crius
	Eco-niche—Move Through Galaxy

In preparing myself for this wonderfully loving step, I have tried to open myself up to unicellular wisdom and DNA collaboration. I have exposed myself, cautiously, to the widest range of geographical, biochemical, interpersonal environments. I have seen every disease, every evil, every taboo, every danger as a form of Hir creativity to be allowed warily, affectionately within my body-brain envelope, so that I can be inoculated and immunized by what my previous ignorance led me to fear or avoid or destroy.

I carry around a little piece of these alien DNA strands in my body-brain, and probably in my DNA itself. And I await the discoveries of the geneticists which will teach us how to increase our symbiotic ability. Is this not the love of all life?

STAGE 22: HERE, and in the two stages to come, we are beyond the objective knowledge of our species; but we can resonate in harmony with the best speculations of our boldest and smartest minds—the quantum physicists. Quarks are probably clusterclouds of information bits defined by the basic coordinates of particles moving through space/time. Of these our material world is made, and can be remade by us. Quantum consumerism is the heady discovery of Heisenberg Determinacy—our brains define the basic nature of nuclear reality.

STAGE 22 **QUANTUM** **CONSUMER**	Zodiac—Sagittarius
	Bio-Structure—Quantum Consumer
	Bio-stage—Singularity
	Tarot—no card
	Trigram—*Chien*-Creative-Heaven
	Divinity—Coeus
	Eco-niche—Move to Galaxy Center

STAGE 23: OUR NUCLEAR FUSION PHYSICISTS have created small stars so that we become gravitational engineers. Our astronomers and gravitational physicists have detected black holes. Our mathematicians have produced equations for fabricating the universe, manipulating fusion and black hole energies. We await with interest the discoveries and technologies which will allow direct translation of our biological-neural equipment to nuclear-atomic form.

STAGE 23 **QUANTUM** **INTELLIGENCE**	Zodiac—Capricorn
	Bio-Structure—Quantum Intelligence
	Bio-stage—Gravitational Engineer
	Tarot—Universe
	Trigram—*Chien*-Creative-Heaven
	Divinity—Lapetus
	Eco-niche—Move to Galaxy Center

OUR MACHINES ARE METAPHORS FOR UNDERSTANDING AND GETTING CONTROL OF OUR BODIES AND BRAINS.

STAGE 24: WHEN WE HAVE DEFINED and translated ourselves into basic particle form we shall link with other like quantum minds in a wonderful, totally revelatory, celebratory fusion. We look forward with delight to that which awaits us on the other side of the gravitational gate. What a wonderful universe we are a part of!

STAGE 24

NEURO-

ATOMIC

FUSION

Zodiac—Aquarius

Bio-Structure—Neuro-Atomic fusion

Bio-stage—Absorbed into Black Hole

Tarot—no card

Trigram—*Chien*-Creative-Heaven

Divinity—Themis

Eco-niche—Center of Galaxy

DO CATERPILLARS KNOW
THEY WILL BECOME
BUTTERFLIES?

CHAPTER 16

SOCIO-BIOLOGICAL MUSINGS

EVOLUTIONARY AGENTS working the frontiers of human hives inevitably make temporary alliances with groups of "outsiders" struggling to present or defend a necessary caste against the disapproval of the gene-pool's conservative inertia.

So it was necessary for me to ally with psychologists against medical psychiatrists, with humanist psychologists against impersonal-experimentalists, with dopers against the police, with leftist militants against mean-spirited conservatives, with Black Panthers against the FBI, with scientists against liberals, with space advocates against Naderites, with geneticists against leftists, with longhairs against the crewcuts, then with Beverly Hills razor-cuts against the indolent hippies; always, always, with the Egg Trust against the Sperm Bank.

LOCATE THE MEMBERS OF YOUR SPECIES AND HANG OUT WITH THEM.

CHANGE

THE REASON FOR THE CONTINUAL SHIFTING of alliances is built into the nature of the change system. The intelligence agent is concerned in the process of continual change. The outcaste groups with which s/he collaborates want, of course, to get inside, become respectable, and push everyone else around.

During the latter days of the 20th Century, the outcaste group that stirred up the most scandal, shock, and subversion of hive morals was "the homosexual." Like other repressed minorities that preceded them, the gays stood up, flexed proud muscles, and rocked the gene-ship. Street-corner newspaper racks that had vended hippie underground papers and Black Panther and radical pressings turned to stocking "alternate lifestyle" newspapers. Gays are the embattled outcaste heroes.

ARE YOU A HIVE-CENTRIST? OR A HIVE OUTCASTE FUTURIST?

THE PARADOX

YOU CAN ONLY BEGIN to de-robotize yourself to the extent that you know how totally you're automated. The more you understand your robothood, the freer you are from it. I sometimes ask people, "What percentage of your behavior is robot?" The average hip, sophisticated person will say, "Oh, 50%." Total robots in the group will immediately say, "None of my behavior is robotized." My own answer is that I'm 99.999999% robot. But the .000001 percent non-robot is the source of self-actualization, the inner-soul-gyroscope of self-control and responsibility.

Of course, there's paradox at every single level of this genetic enterprise. The more freedom you have, the more responsible you have to be. The higher you go, the more precise your navigation must be. I am totally committed to doing something about my own robothood and the robothood of those around me, sending out signals that will activate singularity.

If you're really interested in the mutational sequence of ideas and how they're passed on, old ideas can be fun. For example, in 600 B.C. Buddha was saying things that were as far as you could go in the caste society he came from. His nervous system had advanced 7 or 8 circuits ahead of his time. He simply could not communicate more precisely because he didn't have the technology.

We can be intelligently conscious only in terms of the technologies that we have externalized. Our machines become the metaphors for understanding and getting control of our bodies and brains. Once atomic particles and electronics were discovered, it became possible to apply the Buddhist metaphors.

DE-ROBOTIZATION

WELL, THEN, how does de-robotization take place? Simple: You migrate to ecological niches where the genetically selected intelligence increasers are found. If you are an emerging butterfly, locate the members of your species and hang out with them.

ONE POSSIBILITY IS ROUTINELY OMITTED

-A SUDDEN GLOBAL RAISING OF CONTELLIGENCE.

One possibility might be to simply establishing communication with those persons exhibiting the clearest and most intelligent signals then apparent to you. Trying to do this gets complicated, though, because we are at different stages. Fifty percent of Americans are basically paleolithic and believe in repetitious magic. If you gave the "average American" total political power, s/he'd act like Idi Amin. What sense does democracy make if all members of society are robots from different genetic castes? Each gene-pool produces—just as in a termite colony—exactly the number of caste-workers needed to perform survival functions, which keep changing.

If there's a war and a lot of warrior ants are killed, the queen will produce nothing but warrior ants to balance the colony. Each gene-pool has to produce its warriors, its diggers, its teachers, its artists. If you don't see that all castes are necessary to the whole, it's because you're caught in chauvinisms—the equivalent of worker ants scorning warrior ants.

HUMAN CONDITION

SINCE HOMOSEXUALITY has always been a part of every society, you have to assume that there is something necessary, correct and valid—genetically natural—about it.,

I have been accused of reductionism similar to the the socio-biologist point of view. In chemistry, you have to study the basic elements before you can get the right combinations to create the forms that you want. You are not imposing on the chemicals anything that they don't want. Hydrogen is down there, just ready to start making it with oxygen. Sodium is begging to date chloride. In

order to understand the synergy, you have to reduce
and reduce, but there's no ultimate essence. Even
in the nucleus of the atom, you are confronted
with unique complexities.

Many worry about the human condition. I'm
delighted at the way things are unfolding. Relax.
Evolution is working out on this planet exactly the
way it is supposed to. Anyone living today is being
hurtled through a remarkable historical sequence of
changes. The fact that anyone has survived these
mutations is a ringing endorsement of DNA. So it
makes me smile when anyone starts to come on
with this worry and danger stuff.

FOOL-PROOF

SOME WONDER IF THERE MIGHT BE "cosmic abortion"
of larvals that simply didn't get to the point where
they could migrate off the planet's surface. There is
a question if all such organisms survive to term.
There is one life-organism on this planet, Gaia. Its
shape is spherical—a scum-film on a round rock. Its
very clear aim is to incubate itself and slide over
the entire planet, both watery and terrestrial, and
to continue to push up and out like a vegetative
thing. The whole human species gene-pool represents the neurological aspects of the biosphere. Can
this planetary/spherical biointelligence, called Gaia,
make "mistakes" so that one part of it can destroy
the rest or abort the whole process? Anyone preach-
ing danger, human error, or ecological naughtiness
is talking about him- or herself. Gaia is fool-proof.

Personal philosophies concerned with mortality,
failure, and wickedness lead to generalized projections of doom because each society senses that it is
outmoded. Each society creates agents who jump

ship and create new gene-pools. The future is fearful and gloomy only if you are committed to the current social structure. I'm robot-wired to explore better ways of ship-jumping to carry the Celtic genes into the future.

This leads to continual accusations of treason and betrayal from frightened members of the old gene-pools. My poor, dear Mother didn't understand the very different future into which I was carrying her seed. That's the poignant chagrin—the change-agent helps a genetic jump to the next point, and then evolution moves beyond. My grandfathers moved my seed from Irish medieval bogs to Western Massachusetts. My mother rooted. I continued the migration.

QUANTUM JUMPS IN EVOLUTIONARY INTELLIGENCE.

WE MUST CONSIDER the Gaia hypothesis atmosphere— a unified life-intelligence of which species are simply robot sperm-egg vessels. There is an irreversible logic, a predictable sequence, and a navigational direction to this life-intelligence, and the more you understand its basic principles and rhythms, the better you feel about the whole life situation. You can worry about your own personal situation, and to the extent that you're a hive-centrist rather than a hive-outcaste futurist, you've got a lot to worry about.

> To keep a gene-pool surviving in the present, you have to have a lot of heavy-duty stoics who oppose changes.

For 3,000 years, our most intelligent stoics believed that their social system, therefore everything, was doomed. "All we can do," they said, "is keep our ship going for another generation." Doom/gloom is honorable and genetically necessary. Everything's going exactly according to plan. Hiter and Stalin were important warning signals that everybody picked up. Hiroshima/Nagasaki ended mammalian territorial warfare on a mass scale. So far.

TABOOS

TALKING ABOUT MIND-ALTERING PSYCHEDELICS becomes a new cultural taboo. Taboos are the most fascinating issues in any gene-pool. If you visit another society, you ask, "What are the taboos?" and you locate the genetic tension between the future and the past. Future realities interface with present and past realities at the taboo. Cannibalism, for example, is a taboo against the past. The taboo about LSD wards off the future. It concerns self-directed tampering with your own neurology.

TABOOS OCCUR AT THE INTERFACE OF CHANGE.

MARKING TIME

WELL, SPACE COLONIZATION ISN'T TABOO, YET. In an article in *Mother Jones*, the author states, "Turning to space seems a way of not solving a problem, but evading one."

I'm bored with talking about space colonies, just as I got bored talking about the marijuana legalization. You simply have to wait around until the present left-wing welfare establishment pisses off.

The stay-down-here-and-suffer-equally people can't see that migration is always the way to solve survival problems. So we just sit here marking time until space opens up.

We're being squeezed into space by a genetic imperative, the need to establish new ecological niches for cultural plurality, new solutions, new technologies, lifestyle plurality, consciousness diversification. For example, in not too many years we could have mini-worlds in space made up of just bisexual vegetarians. They can do what they want in their world. That's what evolution is all about—new ecological niches to try our new lifestyles, being smart enough to migrate and not fight. For those who want to change, there will be many worlds of bisexual vegetarians, voting about nudism versus glitter. And their new outcastes will migrate.

HOMOSEXUAL TABOO

I HAVE BEEN ASKED about the neurogenetically programmed functions of gay people. I think they play caste roles in fashion, communication, and outcaste perspectives. Obviously, the gay caste is going to be pushed out of the center of that domesticated nuclear family. They're simply more sophisticated in picking up nonverbal signals, signs, symbols, in seeing through the limitations and vulgarities of the dominant species. So they're going to be the sharpest critics, the best observers. A domesticated father-robot simply isn't going to be looking ahead into the future and predicting alternative societies. On the other hand, you have to understand the irritation of

> TABOOS SPRING FROM THE GENERTIC TENSON BETWEEN THE FUTURE AND THE PAST.

domesticated robots who see this "gay" minority dancing around, heating up the sexual situation with all sorts of campy new twists and making fun of the domesticated. No wonder the poor goodie-goodie, two shoe-types are pissed off.

The gay controversy can be expect to heat up at a period of pre-migration swarming. It is a temporary problem. When we can live for 500 years, kids will grow up knowing that they have endless options for future worlds.

ABORTION TABOO

ALL THESE CULTURAL FRICTIONS WILL DISAPPEAR when space migration allows different castes to build different social realities. Abortion, for example, always becomes an issue just before migration to a new ecological niche. When a territory is underpopulated, DNA turns up the baby-dial. When a niche is overpopulated, DNA turns down the egg-machine and switches on the restless migration buttons. Abortion is unnecessary when we have unlimited real estate in High Orbital Mini-Earths. If you can live for 500 years and build thousands of Plan-Its to fill with people, then no one will mind taking off a century or two to breed 25 kids. More gay people will become wonderful parents when we realize parenthood is a very demanding but brief sequence to pass through.

CLONING

CLONING IS ANOTHER TABOO, scary to terrestrials crowded together on an overpopulated planet. But with unlimited HOMEs being built, cloning will be a natural technique. Nuclear energy is another controversial issue. As soon as solar-satellite power stations start beaming down energy, nukes won't be needed within the atmosphere of the womb-planet. But nukes are needed in high orbit. All taboo controversies occur at the interface of change.

EACH SOCIETY CREATES AGENTS WHO JUMP SHIP AND CREATE NEW GENE-POOLS.

You see, all terrestrials are basically unhappy because we know we are trapped on a prison planet with a short life-span. This tends to make us grumpy, chauvinistic, fearful of change, and suspicious of differences. When we live long enough to build and inhabit many different Plan-its, these new options will ease the horrible terrestrial depressions.

DNA PROGRAMMING

I HAVE BEEN ASKED if I think that we are nearing the point where we will be able to alter the DNA code itself. Well, to the extent that we can alter DNA, we are preprogrammed by DNA to alter it. DNA monitors what happens to it. It's like the center of the midbrain, which is supposed to keep the body temperature at 98.6 degrees. Built-in protection mechanisms assure that as soon as the temperature gets too high, a series of operations go into effect to bring it back down again.

DECIPHERING OF THE DNA CODE INITIATED THE ERA OF GENETIC CONSCIOUSNESS.

No group of humans can interfere with a three-billion-year evolutionary process. The system can break down at the individual level, but that doesn't mean that the

DNA design is in any way invalidated. As a matter of fact, even that breakdown is anticipated. Every entity with the illusion of individuality and free choice can break itself down. The option of individual error is not a problem of free will or determinism, it's both.

DNA'S STRATEGY

However, the strategy of DNA is continually to activate stages prematurely in a few individuals. Different organisms, or different people, can have future-brain circuits activated way ahead of current technology. This accounts for the extraordinary variety of human nervous systems within human society. So it's possible that if you know the fixed, predictable sequence of evolution, you can locate your own gene-pool in the time context.

Every gene-pool or species is a conglomerate mixture of what you'd call the central tendency of the species, plus a lot of the past and some of the future built within it. Consider the American gene-pool just for illustration. I estimate the American gene-pool is now perhaps 50 percent paleolithic or more primitive. Although the average American is a paleolithic caveman monster, the society is happily run by castes more advanced than that. Why? Because the more advanced levels are smarter and can get the powers of transportation and communication.

A STAGE AHEAD

In other words, they can understand how the system works and thereby get to whatever level they aspire to—depending on real understanding, of course. Well, they're one or two steps ahead of the past. The politicians and bureaucrats who shuffle symbols are one step ahead of the average American, who, if you let hir, would just go out and kill and loot and rape. So there is that thin veneer of neurogenetic intelligence that guides gene colonies into the future.

It is kind of like the guidance and control system. I call the guidance and control center of the gene-pool the DOM species. Now ahead of the DOM species, there's a predictable, layered sequence of futique species who are in competition to see which way they are going to move the sperm-egg ship next. And always making up the mass of the gene pool are the swarming neolithic and paleolithic and primate humans who give the biological motive power to the crafts and keep them going. They're the worker ants, the warrior ants.

WE'RE STILL PRIMATES

No matter how advanced, you have in your nervous system the Paleolithic, the primate, the barbarian. So I'm not talking about an elitist "us" against an animalistic "them"— each of us has the whole sequence in our own nervous system. You have to make honest peace with your own reptilian and Paleolithic centers before you can activate future circuits in yourself or signal the realities of those behind or ahead of you.

YOUR NERVOUS SYSTEM CONNTAINS THE PALEOLITHIC, THE PRIMATE, AND THE BARBARIAN.

I intend to sound cold-blooded and impersonal and inhuman. The paradox is this: Your compassion, empathy, and identification with any other form of life depend entirely upon your neurogenetic ability to maintain this evolutionary perspective.

You have to be ultimately inhuman—post-human—to have a shred of intelligent compassion for the freakiness of other human beings. Another paradox is that you can only be as futique and post-terrestrial as you have been successful in dealing with past terrestrial realities. In prison for four years, I had to learn how to master the mammalian savageries that I floated above as a Harvard professor, for example.

FUTIQUE PROPHETS

IT'S EASY TO SEE INTO THE FUTURE. Simply find the futique robots that every gene-pool is throwing up. California is swarming with futique prophets. On the other hand, you can move into the future only as far as you have successfully mastered the past.

WE MUST LINK UP TO CONTINUE THE PROCESS OF OUR OWN EVOLUTION.

Nervous systems activated to future realities 5 or 6 jumps ahead are in danger of losing touch with the present. Sometimes they can't manage an intelligent sexual encounter or even make a living. So it's not just how far into the future you can see, it's how much future can you practically harness to the survival issues in your life right now.

Each human plays the part of a mobile neuron in this emerging organism identified as Gaia. You can also say that a gene-pool is a plexus of neurons, that a solar system is a neural circuit As long as we operate with brains, there's no way that our understanding of the universe can be anything but neurological. We are both limited by and guided by our brain; the brain is always the observational platform from which these maps are being drawn.

I'm a genetic robot—I was programmed to be changeable, which has its risks as well as its advantages.

STAYING OPEN TO CONTINUAL UPDATING BECOMES A NEUROLOGICAL HABIT . . . . . . AFTER A WHILE.

EVOLVE OR DIE!

PAUL DAVIDS IS AN ARTIST AND MOVIE PRODUCER who directed the documentary feature film, *Timothy Leary's Dead*. The DVD includes the 85 minute film with over two hours of additional never-before-seen bonus footage of interviews with Timothy Leary, Baba Ram Dass, and Ralph Metzner, plus Director's Commentary. Paul's other films include *Starry Night*, *Roswell–The UFO Coverup*, starring Martin Sheen and Kyle Maclachlan, and *The Artist & The Shaman*.

The Artist & The Shaman is Paul's personal story of grief and transcendence. Filled with music, art, beauty, and Native American wisdom, the story features a shaman with a cell phone (Rahelio), an artist who paints like van Gogh (Paul Davids), a three-year old genius (Tonatiuh), and the secret writer (Paul's father) who helped President Kennedy win a Pulitzer Prise for *Profiles in Courage*. The lives of these people connect in a quest for deeper meaning as Paul searches, with the help of a modern "medicine man," for the spirit of his departed father among the living in the healing red rock country of Sedona, Arizona. According to critic Bruce Fessier in *The Desert Sun*, this feature documentary is "thumbs up ... a very intimate film ... a journey of self-discovery...."

PAUL DAVIDS

www.pauldavids.com
www.starrynightmovie.com